CW00661651

THREADNEEDLE
JUNE 2009
D. DENAHY 2010

THE FUTURE OF THE BANK OF ENGLAND

A Silver Lining?

Volume II of The Bank of England Bedside Book

The Future of the Bank of England
A Silver Lining?

Volume II of The Bank of England Bedside Book

Published by Medina Publishing Ltd
9 St John's Place
Newport
Isle of Wight PO20 1HL
www.medinapublishing.com

ISBN: 978-0-9567081-2-0 (Hardback)
ISBN: 978-0-9567081-4-4 (Softback)

CIP Data: A catalogue record for this book is available from the British Library

Compiled by Paul Tempest
Drawings by Danny Denahy
Cartoons by Basil Hone
Photographs by Peter Edgley and Stephen Tempest
Designed by Kitty Carruthers
Printed and bound by Toppan Leefung Printing Ltd, China

The opinions and conclusions expressed in this book are those of the author and the individual contributors and do not reflect necessarily those of the Bank of England or anyone else.

THE FUTURE OF THE BANK OF ENGLAND

A Silver Lining?

Volume II of The Bank of England Bedside Book

conceived, compiled and coordinated by

Paul Tempest

including an assemblage of contributions from
The Old Lady of Threadneedle Street (1921–2007)
The Threadneedle Club (founded 1985)
The Threadneedle (founded 2008)

The Way Ahead

Happiness and the Big Picture: Achieving long-term stability despite the squalls from the global economy

Mervyn King

Extracts from a speech given by the Governor of the Bank of England at the Civic Centre, Newcastle, on 25 January 2011

'When it comes to measuring success, don't count money, count happiness.' The advice, not of a Government monitor of our well-being, but Ken Dodd in 1964. Unfortunately, happy is not the word to describe the global economic scene. As Tolstoy might have said: all happy economies are alike; each unhappy economy is unhappy in its own way. [...]

We must not lose sight of the big picture. Large – very large – shocks to relative prices are an inevitable part of the real adjustment vital to the rebalancing of the UK economy. That has led to inflation well above target, and further increases are likely for a few months. None of this means that we cannot return inflation to the target in the medium term, nor that the MPC has abandoned its commitment to meeting the inflation target. Quite the contrary. Attempts to have kept inflation at the target in these circumstances would almost certainly have resulted in even bigger falls in output and higher unemployment, with inflation then falling below target further ahead. [...]

I do not believe that we are about to return to the days before independent central banks ushered in a period of price stability. The Bank of England cannot prevent the squeeze on real take-home pay that so many families are now beginning to realise is the legacy of the banking crisis and the need to rebalance our economy. But we can determine our own inflation rate in the long run, whatever happens in the rest of the world. [...]

The UK economy is well-placed to return to sustained balanced growth over the next few years as a result of a fall in the real exchange rate combined with a credible medium-term path of fiscal consolidation. Of course, there will be ups and downs as the squalls from the world economy blow us around. But the right course has been set, and it is important we maintain it.

CONTENTS

ACKNOWLEDGEMENTS

I would like first to pay tribute to the members of the Threadneedle Club who, over the past 25 years, have provided unfailing support, wise advice and a stream of contributions to the Threadneedle Archive, the *Threadneedle* magazine and this three-volume publishing project.

A special thank you goes to all the good friends, members, family and colleagues who have read through various parts of these books in draft, particularly Peter J Bull, Douglas Croham, Peter Edgley, John Footman, Rodney Galpin, Malcolm Gill, Gavin Gordon, Geoffrey Howe, David Howell, John Keyworth, Angela Knight, Norman Lamont, Nigel Lawson, Kit McMahon, Jeremy Morse, Jacquie Pearce, Max Scott, Tom Stacey, Susie Tempest and David Walker. Also to Kitty Carruthers, now a Director of Medina Publishing, who, with so many good ideas, designed five of my recent hardbacks and a steady stream of booklets for the Threadneedle Club and other purposes.

Two anniversaries fall for me this year. It is 50 years since, in the Chief Cashier's Office, I first began to handle relations with Kuwait and it is 40 years since I completed my 14-month Bank of England secondment in Qatar. Helping develop cordial UK relations with these two states in financial, energy and cultural matters has been a significant thread in my life and I would like to thank the two distinguished current Ambassadors in London, Khaled Al-Duwaisan and Khalid Al-Mansouri for their own part in cementing this enduring friendship.

At home, my wife Jennifer, since Spring 1961, has had to put up with the other woman in my life, a lovingly eccentric old lady, now aged 317. I salute them both with sincere thanks for managing to put up with me with such kindness for such a long time and hope fervently that, for both of them, the best is still to come.

Paul Tempest
Greenwich 00.00.00
January 2011

CONTRIBUTORS

Roger Barnes	*Bishop Bloughram Reflects on the BCCI Trial*
Robert Butt	2007 – *You Are New to the Bank...*
Forrest Capie	*Writing the History of the Bank of England*
Thomas Catto	*From the Governor after the End of the War*
Peter Edgley	*Bank-ese – A Forgotten Dialect?*
Malcolm Gill	*Meetings – A Question of Attitude*
Gavin Gordon	*Sterling and Watermarks*
Barry Hoffmann	*A Great Centenary Victory in Kent*
Geoffrey Howe	*The Abolition of UK Exchange Control*
Mervyn King	*Extracts from Speeches* 2009-11
Angela Knight	*An Innovative Banking Industry*
Norman Lamont	*A New Inflation Target*
Nigel Lawson	*An Independent Bank of England*
Mike Lees	*First Impressions*
Peter Longmuir	*Official Duties with the Discount Houses*
John Lowen	*The Bank for International Settlements*
Jeremy Morse	*First Impressions*
Guy de Moubray	*First Impressions*
Montagu Norman	*The Outbreak of War in* 1939
John Parker	*Hope for a Safe Passage*
Lawrence FT Smith	*Highlights of Two Bag-Carriers*
Roger Stevenson	*First Impressions*
David Walker	*The Best is Yet to Come*
Alan Watson	*As I See It – Building Bridges*

A summer party in the Bank of England garden court, dominated by the St Christopher War Memorial.

Photograph by Peter Edgley

OVERVIEW

The Bank of England has, between 2007 and 2010, survived the greatest crisis in its 317-year history. Doggedly and with considerable skill, it has fought its way day-by-day through intense political and operational pressures, and the impact of huge commercial and financial meltdowns, many of them emanating from overseas and outside its own direct jurisdiction. The Old Lady of Threadneedle Street shows every indication of remaining in good shape to tackle any further crises ahead. Already, it is playing a lead role in the various international financial organisations tackling the long-term issues of central-bank co-ordination, realigned monetary policy, banking reform, a new regulatory framework and how to strengthen global market discipline.

The Shrinkage of the Bank of England Staff

The steep decline in staff numbers from close to 8,000 in 1960 to little more than 1,500 at the low point in 2007 has been halted. The current number is approaching 1,800. A major boost will be the recruitment of staff in 2011–12 to equip the new financial stability division to be established within the Bank as the Prudential Regulation Authority *(see pp. 2,7)*.

The Shrinkage of the Range of Bank Activities

An analysis by the current Bank of England official historian of the period of the 1950s to 1979 demonstrates the wide range of Bank activities compared with the restricted range today *(see pp. 1-4, 6)*.

A Poor Response to Bank Warnings

The devastating scale of the global economic recession of 2007–9 was largely triggered by the banking crisis. The Governor and the Bank had seen it coming: they had observed the abnormal degree of leverage of the banks and the high degree of lending to those who were unlikely to repay. They had signalled that a crisis was possible, but neither the Government, nor the financial sector paid much attention until it was too late *(see pp.6, 9)*.

Changes in Governance in the Bank of England

The recent slimming down of the Court of Directors of the Bank of England from 22 to 12 was said to be justified on efficiency grounds. The response of British industry has been to regret losing its part in this consultative process *(see p. 6 & Annex 2)*.

Impacts on the UK Economy

The banks' response to the liquidity crisis has left the small and medium business sector high and dry, faced with steep rises in borrowing rates, stiffer terms and much greater uncertainty about growth in consumer demand. By the last quarter of 2009, GDP was less than a year earlier; unemployment had soared to 7.8%, mortgage lending to first-borrower customers was approaching standstill, repossessions were rising and a large number of smaller companies were being forced into liquidation *(see pp.10-11)*.

Global Impacts

The collapse of Northern Rock in 2007 revealed acute strain in other UK banks. Simultaneously, the US banks came under intense liquidity pressure. A million US jobs were lost in two weeks. In China, export orders were cancelled and electricity demand, previously growing steadily by 15%, fell abruptly by 8%. In Germany, the value of exports fell abruptly by over 10% and Japanese industrial production fell by 8.5% in a single month *(see pp. 12-13)*.

Longer-Term Impacts on the UK Economy

The scale of quantitative easing and assistance to the banking sector places a heavy additional layer of debt on the UK economy, necessitating increases in taxation and cuts in public sector spending *(see pp.14-16)*.

'Too Important to Fail' – the Reinforced Dominance of the Largest Banks

The extraordinary rate of expansion of the banks was accompanied by the lead banks capturing an increased market share. Asset holdings of the top ten banks in the UK are over 450% of GDP compared with the USA where the top ten banks hold only 60% of GDP *(see pp. 147-50)*.

Other Causes of Global Financial Instability

High current account imbalances of long-standing such as the huge external indebtedness of the USA and the piling up of foreign exchange reserves in China frustrate the balancing of the global payments mechanism and distort the exchange markets. Such imbalances can be alleviated by bilateral and multilateral swap systems provided there is adequate political will and understanding on each side *(see pp. 27-32)*.

The Vulnerability of the Bank of England

Public opinion in the UK assumes that the Bank of England is fully secure for the foreseeable future. Nothing could be further from the truth. Successive British governments have come under repeated pressure from their European Community partners and the EU to jettison sterling in favour of the euro. Once locked in at a fixed rate, the key functions of the Bank of England could be progressively transferred to the European Central Bank. Equally, if a British Government were to decide to take full control of all the Bank's operations, it could do so with the greatest of ease. There is therefore a pressing need for the Bank to explain and defend the substantial economic and political benefits of retaining its independence *(see pp. 81-90)*.

The Bank of England as the Key Global Model for Central Banks

Over the past 14 years, the Bank of England has been able to demonstrate its effectiveness in controlling inflation by the exercise of policy through its Monetary Policy Committee. An analytical capability has been developed and refined to the point where it is second-to-none worldwide. This has been widely admired and copied elsewhere. Over the past five years, the Bank of England Centre for Central Banking Studies has provided training and seminars at home for the staff of well over 100 other central banks and runs over 25 regional and other seminars and workshops overseas each year *(see pp.21-6 & Annex 6)*.

A Reshaping of Banking Regulation is in Progress

When Banking Regulation is transferred back to the Bank of England on the demise of the Financial Services Authority (FSA) in 2012, an opportunity is presented to slim down the mechanistic hard-edge of the FSA and to restore the thoughtful, intuitive face-to-face relationships that lie at the heart of effective banking supervision *(see pp. 35-6 & 142-4)*.

Corporate Governance in the UK Financial Sector

In most of the problem banks over the past three years, the function of the non-executive directors to provide a check on the decisions of the chief executive and other executive directors had largely fallen into abeyance. Many of the non-executive directors proved ignorant of the details of the business and had been sidelined from the decision-making process. There is therefore a need for a thorough revision of the role of the non-executive director and a redefinition of his or her accountability *(see pp. 142-4)*.

The City of London Expects a Swift Rebound

With the European Commission intent on elaborating its own bank supervision directives, and eurozone policy pre-occupied with providing interim finance to the weaker members, the attractiveness of London as the premier financial centre has begun to reassert itself with some renewed interest to open new overseas banks and to place more international business through London *(see pp. 163-8)*

PREFACE

Volume One – A Thread of Gold

Volume 1 of *The Bank of England Bedside Book* was published in October 2008 with the subtitle, *A Thread of Gold*. It aimed to encapsulate something of the history and spirit of the Bank of England from its foundation in 1694 to mid-2008.

Over the past half-century, the Bank of England has shrunk to one-fifth of its former size. During that period, the Bank has undergone immense change and within the last five years experienced a further redefinition of its governance and core functions and objectives. A decision in 1997 by the incoming Labour Government granted independence in setting interest rates to the Bank of England through its new Monetary Policy Committee (MPC). For almost ten years, the MPC was able to stabilise inflation at close to the Government target rate of 2 percent per annum. At the same time, responsibility for banking and financial sector supervision was transferred from the Bank of England to a new public sector entity, the Financial Services Authority (FSA) whose staff grew rapidly to double that of the Bank. The UK was left with a weakened mechanism to cope with the market collapse and major bank failures that have characterised the last five years. As a result the Bank became less close to the activities of the City of London but has, through its 12 new regional agencies, greatly strengthened its understanding of the UK economy, employment and industry.

In terms of global economics and politics, the Bank's standing as a role-model and as a highly-valued player in international financial and economic cooperation is unimpaired. Shortly after the new Conservative-Liberal Government took office in 2010, it announced its intention to dismantle the FSA and to transfer back to the Bank of England direct responsibility for supervision of the banking sector.

Themes explored briefly in Volume I and developed in Volume II include:

- The continuing need for the Bank to collaborate closely with the Government both in day-to-day operations and in long-term objectives.

- The major opportunity presented to the Bank to help promote the UK financial sector and City of London financial services at home and overseas.

- The need for the Bank of England to re-establish its historic leadership role in the supervision and regulation of the UK financial sector.

- The need for a long-term recruitment, training, motivation and promotion strategy within the Bank.

- Much more effort is needed to inform the markets, the media and the general public of the role of the Bank within the national economy.

- Repeatedly challenged by the aspirations of the European Central Bank to exercise greater control of the Bank of England and for the replacement of sterling by the Euro, the Bank needs a more coherent long-term strategy for its survival and for a valuable independent role within the European region.

- Wide opportunities are emerging to strengthen ties with other central banks and international agencies worldwide.

From the Introduction to Volume One – A Thread of Gold

'In the world at large, confidence in the Bank of England remains unshaken. In a troubled and unstable world economy and increasingly globalised markets, the issues of business integrity, employee motivation and involvement are still relevant.

"My word is my bond"
"The lender of last resort"
"As safe as the Bank of England"

All these concepts have been widely known, admired and respected worldwide for over three centuries, a thread of gold through our history. We need to know that this precious thread will be there for our future.'

Final paragraph of the Introduction to Volume 1

From the Conclusions to Volume One – A Thread of Gold

'The most pressing priority is for the Bank of England to continue to evolve. Just how the doors might be thrown open in the quest for a new and open public face, a new and friendly image for the new tasks ahead, rests essentially with the Governors and Directors. The important thing is that when the decision-makers and general public worldwide think of the Bank of England, they have firmly printed in their minds, much more than that of a fortress or museum image of the past, but also a firm impression of continuity of purpose and a coherent, well-rounded, well-argued vision of the future.'

Final paragraph of the Conclusions to Volume I

Volume Two – A Silver Lining?

Volume Two – A Silver Lining? presents an alternative view of the future of the Bank of England, otherwise condemned, on the recent rate of shrinkage, to extinction within little more than a decade. It begins with an analysis of what has been going on over the last five years and then identifies what makes the Bank so special to the UK financial sector, to the European economy in general and as a lead central bank of impeccable standing to this day.

Volume 2 looks at how, in the past, the Bank of England has responded to some major challenges and formulated its own policy on how to develop a framework for the future which stimulates private enterprise, investment, trade and growth. The Bank was not always successful. It made some serious mistakes and often, as a consequence, it either fell out with the government of the day or seriously alienated the opinion of the City of London. From time to time, including quite recently, it succeeded in doing both. But even in the bad times, the Bank of England has relied on robust mechanisms and accountable commercial and legal practice to provide sound responses of great long-term value and to earn the respect of all those who recognise the need for a strong and durable pivot in the national, regional and global economy.

Defining the National Interest

The continuing strength of the Bank of England derives therefore from the 317-year experience of holding the middle ground between the seething multiple ferment of trade and commerce and the ever-grasping, directing hand of government. The secret to its success lies in that the solutions it arrives at and the reconciliation it achieves have to be, over the long-term, broadly acceptable to the British public in general. What is distilled in this process is a valuable analysis of where the long-term national interest lies in an environment where the planning range of any government can be eroded to what remains of the five-year electoral span and where the attention of a City dealer bidding in a highly competitive environment can from time to time be measured in a few days, a few hours, sometimes a few minutes and, at the point of closure, to a few seconds.

The Principle of the Lifeboat

The source of the strength of the Bank of England lies in a mastery of always knowing what is going on, whether in government or within the UK financial community or worldwide. This is not so much a matter of shuffling paper and much more one of knowing the key corporations and personalities involved. Thus forewarned in good time of impending trouble and shipwreck, the Bank of England lifeboat has to be fully equipped at all times to go to sea with clear instructions as to its purpose and appropriate remedy – short-term relief and/or long-term salvage.

A Global Player

Finally, *A Silver Lining?* looks to the current and impending strains in the global economy and international financial system. Where might the Bank of England be of greatest value and potential? Here, I think, there has been a marked absence of positive thinking. This short book cannot, of course, deliver the answers, but, if it does nothing else, it can begin to ask some of the right questions.

The Old Lady and Threadneedle

To illuminate the above issues, we draw on articles and comment in the Bank's own quarterly internal magazine, *The Old Lady of Threadneedle Street* (1921 to December 2007) and to its independent annual successor, since June 2008. *Threadneedle* is the new name for the journal of the Bank's alumni organisation, the Threadneedle Club founded in 1985, and now in 2011, some 600 strong, all of whom have worked in some capacity or other in the Bank of England.

How did the various Governors (only nine in the last 90 years) respond to crisis? Here, in their various public speeches and *Old Lady* interviews and Threadneedle Club talks and speeches are useful clues to the pattern of their thinking. How did the Bank provide warnings to the staff of imminent upheaval? Sometimes, as illustrated, the warnings were embedded in *Old Lady* editorials. Sometimes in specially commissioned feature articles, more often than not, in the wit of *Flyleaf* which was founded by *The Old Lady* in 1932 as a safety valve for dissention and is still a feature of *Threadneedle* today. How is this strong *esprit de corps* reinforced today? How do other central banks view the Bank of England today? How easily can they read this vital sub-text accurately as a positive global message of long-standing goodwill?

WARNING: This volume does not follow a strict chronological order in analysing the events of 2007–11.

- For the 14 key topics covered, see Overview on pages xi–xiv.
- For the 14 key conclusions, see Part Fifteen on pages 175–87.
- The Summary Index to Volume Two on page 199 provides a useful route to key personalities, lead contributors, major institutions and relevant events.

Volume Three – A Copper Bottom

The third volume in this trilogy about the Bank of England will be published in 2013. It will bring the story up-to-date with a focus on 2011–3 and will provide a completely different sort of thread through the history of the Bank of England and particularly through the last 50 years. Volume Three will focus specifically, as the title implies, on fully protecting this venerable and immensely valuable ship-of-state. The issue of criminality cannot be disregarded. Terrorism, guarding against armed attacks, protecting the gold, institutional skulduggery, money-laundering; forgery, fraud, theft, infiltration by spies, improperly conducted intelligence operations, insider trading, blackmail, perjury, murder, market conspiracies, civil unrest, hijacks, ransoms, all demand, increasingly today, a reliable rapid response mechanism. Again this third volume will be richly enlivened by the personal contributions of Threadneedle Club members, particularly their experiences and stories from the Nightly Watch which was instituted in 1809, a delayed reaction to the Gordon Riots of 1780, that operated every night until 1994 when mobiles, laptops, bleepers and an expanded team of mainly professional ex-policemen took over. Add to this our detailed researches in the Bank archives and the 20,800 pages of *The Old Lady* and the whole adds up to a hitherto barely-known story packed with interest and surprise. The Conclusions suggest how a much more vigorous mechanism of international co-operation, where the Bank of England plays a significant role, might begin to provide vital new safeguards for the future.

SOME CONTRIBUTORS TO VOLUME ONE – A THREAD OF GOLD

Roger Barnes; John Bartlett; Sir George Blunden; Peter J Bull; Mike Clancy; Pamela Clayton; Frank Dancaster; Graham Dunbar; Guy de Moubray; Peter Edgley;David Fecci; Malcolm Gill; Garth Hewitt; Pen Kent; Sir Kit McMahon; Sir Jeremy Morse; Lord O'Brien; Jacquie Pearce; Richard Powers; Lord Richardson; Jasper Rootham; Tim Smith; Paul Tempest; Keith Wood.

CHAPTER HEADINGS OF VOLUME ONE

Preface: Bleak House; Hard Times; Great Expectations; A Christmas Carol

- Some Landmarks 1694–2008; Esprit de Corps
- Chief Cashier's Office 1809–1989
- Carrying the Bag to Basle 1930–2008
- The Overseas Office; Travel, Assignments and Adventures Overseas
- The Nightly Watch since 1780; Guarding the Gold
- The Bank of England Sports Club 1908–2008
- The Bank of England Sailing Club 1975–2008
- *The Old Lady of Threadneedle Street* 1921–2007
- The Bank of England Literary Awards 1950–90
- The Threadneedle Club founded 1985; *Threadneedle* founded 2008
- Kenneth Grahame and *The Wind in the Willows*, 1908
- The Manila Bill, 1763

Conclusions: Shrinkage; Access; the Mediatory Role; A Vital Asset

SOME COMMENTS ON VOLUME ONE

Published October 2008

"It is written beautifully."

Mervyn King

"Sandwiched between a thoughtful introduction and conclusion ... a charming, affectionate and eminently readable pot pourri."

Nigel Lawson

"A valuable portrayal of the Bank of England – coming at a time when a better understanding of the Bank, and its central role in the financial integrity and success of the United Kingdom was never more necessary. Recent events have shown how unwise it was to diminish the powers and position of the Bank of England in City affairs. This book is a first balanced step towards re-thinking the regulatory hiving-off decision and making the UK's entire financial structure and operation once again 'as safe as the Bank of England'."

David Howell

Nine Governors in Ninety Years

Montagu Collet Norman	24 years	1920–44
Thomas Sivewright Catto	5 years	1944–49
Cameron Fromanteel Cobbold	12 years	1949–61
Rowland Stanley George Baring The Earl of Cromer	5 years	1961–66
Leslie Kenneth O'Brien	7 years	1966–73
Gordon William Humphreys Richardson	10 years	1973–83
Robert (Robin) Leigh-Pemberton	10 years	1983–93
Edward Alan John George	10 years	1993–2003
Mervyn Allister King	from 2003	

To complete the list for the last century, it is necessary to add:

Alfred Clayton Cole	1911–13
Walter Cunliffe	1913–18
Brien Cokayne	1918–20

Introduction

Writing the History of the Bank of England

Forrest Capie

Professor Capie's The Bank of England 1950s–1979 *was published by Cambridge University Press in November 2010. Below is the text of his remarks to the Threadneedle Club in October 2009.*

Thank you for the invitation and the opportunity to say a few words about writing the history of the Bank. It is a great pleasure to be here. It has also been a great pleasure as well as a considerable challenge writing the latest addition to the Bank's history, just recently completed. As you will all know the Bank had a long history of being closed, secretive, and even obstructive. Some say the inward–looking building is itself something of a metaphor. One frustrated author trying to comment in the 1930s wrote, 'the Bank of England has been since its foundation . . . a private and long-sustained effort in lucrative mumbo-jumbo'. Anyone making enquiries from outside was rebuffed. The beginnings of change then came as a major anniversary loomed (the 250th) and the Bank commissioned its history for the first time. The commissioning continued. The present Governors have a serious interest in history and even advocate its use in approaching contemporary problems and it was the Governor who took the most recent initiative to bring the history up to 1979.

The history of the Bank should be about what the Bank did (and how, and why, and with what consequences if it is possible to say). In the period from the 1950s to 1980 the Bank did a lot of things, many of them far removed from the two core purposes that fill most of its time today.

In the third quarter of the twentieth century the Bank: managed the government's debt; ran the EEA for the Treasury; administered exchange controls; was the agent in the gold market; interfaced with the IMF and other international bodies; was responsible for the note issue; ran the City; represented the City to government; directed bank lending; rescued companies both financial and non-financial; dabbled in finance for industry; promoted central banking around the world; conducted supervision of the banking system, albeit lightly and informally; operated in the money markets; for most of the time did a minimal amount of economic research; and constantly nagged and annoyed the Chancellor of the Exchequer on public spending. Not much hint in there of monetary policy as currently understood. But a history of the Bank is a history of what they did and that is what they did. The numbers employed give some indication of the differences between then and now. In 1960 there were around 8,000 employees in the Bank. Today there are around 1,700. But in 1960 there were only 2.5 economists while today there are about 300 – a change in ratio from roughly 1:3000 to 1:6. Incidentally, the half economist was the Deputy Governor, Humphrey Mynors, who had taught economics at Cambridge in the 1930s but was said to have a horror of two words, economics and research.

The writing of history is, of course, in part determined by current interests, so it would be expected that histories written over the next decade will be more interested than before in financial stability. In the 1950s and 1960s there was stability and no one was writing or talking about it or supervision. But then instability reappeared in the 1970s.

A challenge for the historian is finding the appropriate primary material. When the central bank has enjoyed a long period of private ownership and carried out normal banking business it has undoubtedly acquired all the habits of secrecy that go with that. These mean many things for the historian. One is that many of the most important decisions did not get recorded. Decisions were arrived at orally among a small group and by their nature were highly sensitive and not written down. Major business was conducted at 'Books' every day with the Governor and his senior officials. Before the 1980s no records were kept of these meetings.

Thus much of interest never got recorded and then some of what *was* recorded never reached the archive. And even after that there will be loss from damage and other kinds of destruction be they accidental or deliberate. For example, when the Bank's archive was to be brought back to the head office from Roehampton just ten years ago, 100 tons of ledgers were destroyed. This was regarded by the archivist of the time as something of a triumph, reducing as it did the storage requirements by 1.8 kilometres of shelving. But it left no trace of private customers' accounts from 1900 to 1970.

In this period the Bank made no pretence of being intellectual. If anything it was anti-intellectual ('a bank not a study group' was a popular phrase frequently used). But from the late 1960s the Bank was increasingly forced to defend itself and had to employ more economists to do that. After that there was growing internal discussion that produced paper, on the importance of money, on monetary control, on monetary targeting, and on other possible techniques of control. The same went for the exchange rate and exchange-rate policy. And much of that paper was kept.

The absence of primary material can to some extent be substituted for with other archival material and in as many other ways as possible such as diaries and memoirs where feasible, though few Bank employees admit to keeping these. For some topics use can be made of oral history

– interviewing the participants – and while that has been an enjoyable and rewarding exercise it comes with major cautions. At any rate, on the strength of the material found the challenge is to produce an accurate account of what the Bank did, and how, and why, and with what consequences. If all of that can be done the next challenge is to make it readable and possibly even bring a smile to the face of the reader occasionally – a real challenge when describing the workings of the gilt market or the pros and cons of forward intervention in the foreign exchange markets. But it might be of interest to you to know that you will find in the index: Donald Bradman, Che Guevara (governor of the central bank of Cuba in 1962), Tarzan, and the Mafia. Actually the reference to the Mafia has been removed on health and safety grounds – my health and my safety.

Note: HISTORIES OF THE BANK

The first formal History of the Bank of England was commissioned in the 1930s to mark the Bank's 250th Anniversary in 1944. It was written by Sir John Clapham, Professor of Economic History at the University of Cambridge and covered the period 1694 to 1914.

The second formal History of the Bank was compiled by Richard Sayers, Professor of Monetary Economics at the London School of Economics and covered the period 1891 to 1944.

The third History was written by John Fforde, former Chief Cashier and Executive Director of the Bank and covered the period 1945 to 1950.

The fourth History by Professor Forrest Capie covered the period 1950 to 1979 and was published in November 2010 by Cambridge University Press.

At a less formal level, the Governors also commissioned or gave their blessing and approval of the text to several other popular Histories of which the three most successful were by John Francis (1847,) Marston Acres (1931) and Elizabeth Hennessy (1992).

Hope for a Safe Passage

Sir John Parker

Report on the 2009 Annual Threadneedle Dinner

From the report by Gavin Gordon published in Threadneedle *of June 2010 covering the Annual Dinner held on 22 October 2009 in The HAC, London EC1*

Rodney Galpin welcomed everyone to the 24th Annual Dinner and remarked upon the historic military record and impressive surroundings of the Honourable Artillery Company. He conveyed the best wishes of the Governor who was committed to an engagement elsewhere.

Between courses, Chris Webb, both a member of the Club and a long-standing member of the HAC, outlined the long history of the HAC since its foundation by Henry VIII in 1537, making it the oldest regiment of the British Army of today.

Professor Forrest Capie, who has just completed the manuscript of his history of the Bank from 1950 to 1979 (published by Cambridge University Press in July 2010) explained what a pleasure and challenge it had been. He had found, to his surprise, that not very much of relevance to his task had been recorded within the Bank and that what was recorded was in a particular mumbo-jumbo that made it difficult to understand or interpret ... The task of discovering what had happened in the Bank before 1980 was complicated by the destruction of 100 tons of ledgers and other material when the Bank vacated the Bank of England Record Office at Roehampton.

The Deputy Governor then introduced Sir John Parker, just retired as Chairman of the Court of the Bank of England over the previous five years. Charlie Bean described him as 'director of everything' within the Bank and gave an awesome catalogue of appointments outside.

John Parker explained that he came from Northern Ireland and a background in engineering, shipbuilding and shipping, which he has always regarded as a great indicator of global economic health. Currently, freight rates for container ships had collapsed and 15 percent of the global stock of such ships were laid up. Shipping carries 93 percent of world trade and has witnessed a 30 percent fall in trade volumes at the trough. Recovery will therefore take some time.

On the current crisis, John Parker asked whether anyone saw it coming. The Governor and the Bank had, in his view, seen it. They had signalled clearly that a crisis was looming and had stressed the foolishness of high leverage and of lending too much to those who have little capacity to repay. Many banks serve the nation well, yet others lend beyond normality and need to be deterred from taking on excessive risk.

Mariners constantly assess risk. It is time to reassess values throughout the economy. Under the mature guidance of the Bank, the British people and the British economy can and will recover. He hoped for a safe passage and calmer seas in 2010.

In summing up his five years with the Bank of England, he felt that while the Bank's Court was a splendid powerhouse of skills and fit for purpose, the rejection of engineers at board level in preference to financiers is done within the commercial environment at our peril.

Numbers employed in the Bank in 1960 were, he understood, around 8,000 staff with three economists. Today there are 1,700 with 300 economists, well over 1 in 6 of the total staff. He outlined some of the consequences of persistent change on this scale.

Sir John Parker was Chairman of the Court of the Bank of England from 2004 to 2009. He has been Chairman of the National Grid since 2002 and chairman of Anglo-American plc since following a most distinguished career in shipping and shipbuilding. He was Managing Director of Austin-Pickersgill, Sunderland in 1974-8, Chairman and Chief Executive of Harland & Wolff in 1983-93 and Chairman of Babcock International in 1994-2000. He lists his recreations as reading, ships, sailing and music.

"Economists need faith, hope and clarity.
The greatest of these is clarity."

Mervyn King, Governor since 2003

The Answer is 23

Mervyn King
at the Lord Mayor's Banquet for Bankers and Merchants of the City of London at the Mansion House on 16 June 2010

'Let me now return to the quiz question I posed earlier – to what question is 23 the answer? Several plausible answers come to mind. First, 23 is the number of players in England's World Cup squad in South Africa. Second, it is of course 23 years since England last won the Ashes 'down under'. But neither of these is the right answer which is that 23 years is the age difference between the Chancellor of the Exchequer and the Governor of the Bank of England. In case there is any doubt, George is the younger. This age difference is highly desirable because the appropriate incentives are to allocate the responsibility of determining monetary policy to the older generation, which has a real interest in preserving the value of money, and the responsibility for fiscal policy to the younger generation, on whom falls the burden of excessive debt. If we are tempted to leave a large burden of debt for the next generation to pay back, what better incentive mechanism than to have as Chancellor someone who has a longer life expectancy than any previous Chancellor on record? Given those incentives, Chancellor, I look forward to a harmonious coordination of monetary and fiscal policy.'

PART ONE

'Like Falling Off a Cliff' 2007–9

The unprecedented scale and viciousness of the global banking and financial crisis over the three years 2007 to 2009 has engulfed the global economy and delivered shock-waves which have profoundly changed our perceptions of the prospects for global economic growth and our confidence in the stability and resilience of the international financial system. It has been, announced the Governor, Mervyn King, like falling off a cliff.

The Bank of England had been expressing increasing concern about some of the structural changes in banking and financial sector supervision over recent decades. It had also formulated its misgivings about a steeply rising trend in liquidity and in bank credit, particularly in the United States and the United Kingdom and it had warned the UK Government and others repeatedly about the risks of commercial banks bundling dubious mortgage assets and about recent legislation which freed them from obligations to structure their assets to provide sound protection for their customers, notably householders with a mortgage and small businesses. Here was a system which had worked more or less efficiently and safely in the United Kingdom for over a century being placed in jeopardy.

A Credit Drought for Small and Medium Businesses

On 28 July 2010, the Governor testified before the Treasury Select Committee that the reluctance of British banks to lend to the small and medium business sector was causing substantial and lasting damage to the British economy. Reinforcing his pleas of January 2009 ('I fully understand the sense of injustice that small business must feel about being held hostage by the banks'), he explained how many businesses that had had the same banking relationship for 60 to 80 years had been suddenly, out of the blue, faced with a letter, churned out by a computer, demanding very steep increases and sometimes a doubling or more of borrowing rates. Since then the financial press has been packed with contributions from small and medium-sized companies confirming the arbitrary treatment handed out by the banks they thought they knew well and trusted. The overall statistics are devastating. In 2009 19,908 UK companies went into liquidation; a further 4,161 went into administration. The pace of business collapse did not slacken in the first quarter of 2010, when a further 4,456 companies went into liquidation, leading to what the Governor called a 'heart-breaking situation' for such 'a seed-bed sector' on which the country relied for an economic turnround. The UK faced, he said, a long haul in its journey to recovery. A short lull in the second quarter in the level of liquidations seemed by end-July 2010 to have petered out. By May 2010 total net lending to companies had fallen by another £2.3 billion, the third month of declines.

Mervyn King dismissed the claims of the banks that their lending had declined on account of lack of demand. He complained about banks paying out large amounts of dividends or compensation to employees through a period when they had undertaken to build up their capital 'buffers'. The British Bankers Association responded with a promise to review what was going on at present in detail and agreed with the Governor that more competition in the credit sector would mean more choice for bank customers and that alternative sources for business funding were urgently needed and should be actively explored.

The First Signs of Collapse

The first intimation that there was serious trouble ahead came from France and Germany in August 2007 when BNP Paribas reported 'a complete evaporation of liquidity in certain market segments of the US securitization market' and, instantly, froze several of its major funds. The European Central Bank in Frankfurt was obliged the same day to pour a colossal sum, close to Euro 100 billion, into the markets in an attempt to bring down overnight inter-bank lending rates that had rocketed sky-high. Despite some alleviation, the panic had quickly been transmitted worldwide and several other European banks led by IKB in Germany collapsed.

In London, the markets were in serious disarray. The first casualty was the collapse of Northern Rock, a bank with a rapidly rising mortgage portfolio and, as was then discovered, a heavy reliance on short-term wholesale funding, part of it of US origin. The Bank of England poured in some £30 billion but in vain. News spread rapidly that Northern Rock was going under and long queues of deposit-holders appeared outside every one of their branches. With them came the affected mortgage-holders and other demonstrators, some of a more extreme political persuasion, who were observed on television nightly by an anxious general public. The press was quick to claim that this was the first run on a major bank in the United Kingdom for over 150 years. For the Government, matters seemed to be running out of their control and it was decided that the only viable solution was to nationalise Northern Rock.

In the United States, the Federal Reserve Bank injected massive liquidity into the market and declared itself ready to accept a much wider range of collateral. Events moved swiftly with increasing panic among the banks and the public. In March 2008, a previously blue-chip specialised banking corporation, Bear Sterns had to be rescued by a heavily discounted sale to JP Morgan. Through the summer further crises and failures came thick and fast in both Europe and the United States and very many banks and financial institutions signalled that they were under acute pressure. By September 2008, the insurance group AIG was rescued with some difficulty, but no such solution could be found for the collapse of Lehman Brothers which declared bankruptcy. At this point the viability of the entire global financial system appeared to be on a knife-edge.

The Plunge into Recession

The impacts of this unprecedented evaporation of business and consumer confidence worldwide were quickly picked up. Global equity prices had, within one month, fallen disastrously. The key global indicators of economic prosperity were flashing danger signals. Already in October 2008 the Baltic Dry Index, a key indicator of the demand for shipping space worldwide, had fallen at the fastest pace on record. Shipping carries 93 percent of world trade. Freight rates for container ships collapsed and very quickly 15 percent of total world container capacity was being laid up. The volume of goods and materials moved by ship fell by 30 percent at the trough. Round the world new shipping orders were terminated or placed on hold and as completions were accelerated, completed or abandoned, shipyards fell silent. The sheer scale of this abrupt downturn could not be checked and the consensus assumption of continuing global economic growth of 3 percent per annum was almost immediately downgraded to, at most, +1 percent per annum with a strong possibility of nil or negative growth for some years to come.

In China, electricity production, hitherto expanding steadily at +15 percent per annum fell in November 2008 by 8 percent over November 2007 – the steepest fall on record. In the USA, one million jobs were lost in the space of two months, November to December 2008: nothing on this scale had been seen for over 60 years. Industries worldwide took note and scaled back investment as quickly as they could. In Germany, the value of exports fell by over 10 percent, while in Japan industrial production fell by 8.5 percent in a single month.

Quantitative Easing

The scale and shock of this potentially catastrophic downturn had a profound psychological effect. All over the world, governments which had relied hitherto on self-regulation within the private-sector and on free market forces to eliminate the weaklings or blackguards who stepped out of line, were faced with unprecedented pressure to prop up ailing economies. Investment was placed on hold; recruitment dried up; aid obligations and social subsidies were placed under review. The future looked grim.

Governments responded by cuts in interest rates, huge fiscal injections and the provision of the equivalent of hundreds of billions of dollars in capital and funding to support banks. The long-term consequences of straining budgets and the economy by having to pay off these massive new government debts became immediately apparent. As Mervyn King, Governor of the Bank of England, put it, with characteristic dryness, in a speech given to the Confederation of British Industry in January 2009;

'The scale and urgency of their actions embodied an audacity born out of pessimism.'

A Specific Dilemma for the UK

The UK, with a million jobs at stake in the financial sector alone, came under particularly heavy fire. Commercial property prices plummeted. Repossessions and redundancies soared. The steep increase in unemployment unsettled business sentiment and placed rising costs on the welfare budgets. Interest rates approached zero, making it necessary for the Government to initiate 'quantitative easing' – buying, on a vast scale, commercial or government securities directly to increase money supply. There were huge new surprises on the high street. By spring 2008 the British Government had taken majority stakes in the Royal Bank of Scotland and a new bank created by the merger of Lloyds TSB (Trustee Savings Bank) and Halifax Bank of Scotland. Rumours of further mergers and nationalisations were rife.

Who Was to Blame?

The finger of blame was pointed, not surprisingly, first and foremost at those major banks that had collapsed. Here was a target worthy of attack. Was it their greed or incompetence or both? Much was made of the new incentive and bonus culture which encouraged their dealers to take excessive risk. The personal rewards for success were grotesque by comparison with almost any other business sector. Some of the bank chairmen and boards of directors had also rewarded themselves with salaries, pension rights, equity options and other perks on a hitherto unheard-of scale. Yet these custodians of our future appeared to have largely abandoned traditional banking prudence in favour of short-term greed. While the financial pie was growing faster than the real economy, there was little problem and even less awareness of risk or of the damage that might be inflicted on the wider economy. On re-examination, it became clear that many of the chairmen, directors and senior management had little understanding of the complex instruments into which their dealers were buying and the high exposure of largely unregulated inter-bank trading. They had not spotted that a huge gap had emerged between the nominal value of the derivative instruments they were using and the real value of their underlying assets. Even in 2007 the size of what was known as the 'credit default swap market' had risen to over $40 trillion without the banks or the regulators or their governments batting much more than an eyelid.

So the finger of blame moved next to the ratings agencies which had expanded very fast with the fat fees paid by the banks for AAA (triple A) ratings for new lucrative security issues. These agencies, in a state of collapse or near-collapse, turned to their governments for help who, in turn, passed the buck to the official regulators of the financial markets.

The regulators received very short shrift from the media and general public. They had been very slow and ill-equipped to respond to what was happening. They pleaded, with some justification, that they were powerless to prevent the under-capitalisation of the banks when the markets collapsed. It was clear that some of the major regulatory authorities had been so baffled by what was happening that they were unwilling to act at all. The Emperors of high-rise regulation and their huge new battalions of statisticians and officials had been well and truly caught without their clothes.

Why had this been allowed to happen? Who were the politicians who could be blamed for such a debacle? In the United States it was the government who had sponsored specialised agencies such as Freddie Mac and Fanny May to assist poorer families to borrow more. This government involvement had greatly stimulated the excessive growth of the sub-prime mortgage market. The link was undeniable and closely related to the explosive growth of bank credit and a real-estate bubbling of house prices.

Where were the lead central banks in all this? Most of them pointed to the fact that their prime focus was on domestic monetary policy – the responsibility of holding inflation within an agreed limit by setting domestic interest rates and intervening actively whenever necessary in the money market. Allied to this was an ill-defined wish for stability in the financial sector and a responsibility to monitor and, if necessary, smooth exchange rates. As far as bank regulation was concerned, the Federal Reserve Bank, the European Central Bank and the Bundesbank and the Bank of Japan were quick to point out that the responsibility for bank supervision was vested elsewhere and that, in any case, much of the credit expansion which had triggered the economic boom had taken place outside the regulated system and where the investment banks specialising in derivatives could operate with relative impunity.

The Rise and Fall of the FSA

In the United Kingdom, there had been a similar bubbling of house prices, but there was another factor of acute political sensitivity. To the amazement of many, the new Labour Government had arrived in 1997 with two fundamental pieces of new legislation – the creation of a new independent Monetary Policy Committee within the Bank of England to set interest rates and the establishment of a Government-controlled Financial Services Authority to take over banking and other financial sector supervision.

Neither of these two measures was entirely new in concept. Indeed in papers in the late 1980s (see Part 8), the Conservative Chancellor, Nigel Lawson, had pointed out the value of easing the burden on the Treasury and Government, by giving the Bank of England wider independent powers. He had also foreseen the risk of the Bank of England getting clogged up with minor regulatory obligations and quoted the example of Germany, where banking supervision was very successfully vested in the Government-run *Bundesaufsichtsamt* in Berlin. Yet nowhere had he envisaged throwing the baby out with the bath-water by suggesting a mechanism whereby the Bank of England became isolated from the regulatory authority and also from the City and thereby lost the forewarning and flexibility to intervene with discretion whenever a bank or other major financial institution got into trouble.

Yet the Bank of England did respond as promptly, discreetly and effectively as it could. In November 2009 it disclosed for the first time that it had provided £61.6 billion of emergency liquidity assistance to two major banks, HBOS and RBS at the height of the crisis in November 2008. Without that assistance those institutions would not have survived.

With the arrival of the new Conservative-Liberal Coalition Government in 2010, the new Prime Minister, David Cameron and Chancellor of the Exchequer, George Osborne lost no time in announcing the break-up of the FSA and the return to the Bank of England of the key powers of banking supervision, giving an immediate strengthening of intelligence and intervention.

The Overhaul of Financial Supervision and Regulation

At end-July 2010 flesh was put on these decisions affecting more than 100,000 businesses in the UK. The Government published plans for a radical overhaul of the supervisory system as applied to the whole financial sector.

- The Prudential Regulation Authority (PRA) will be formed as a division of the Bank of England. It will have primary responsibility for up to 2,000 banks and other lead financial institutions in the City.

- The Consumer Protection and Markets Authority (MPMA) will take over the task of monitoring and regulating the activities of some 99,000 firms regulated hitherto by the Office of Fair Trading.

The design and implementation of all these measure are to be vested in a new Bank of England committee, 11-strong, to be called The Financial Policy Committee (FPC) under the chairmanship of the Governor. Six of the members of the FPC will be Bank of England staffers. The Treasury has estimated the cost of the transition to the PRA, CPMA and FPC at £50 million spread over three years and all to be recovered from the finance industry through the imposition of higher levies.

Eight Strategic Priorities of the Bank of England in 2010–20

(as endorsed by the Court of the Bank of England and explained in detail in the Bank of England's 2010 Annual Report dated May 2010).

1. Keep inflation on track to meet the 2 percent target, and sustain support for the monetary policy framework and the benefits of low inflation.
2. Ensure the Bank has the policies, tools and infrastructure in place to implement monetary policy, provide liquidity insurance to the banking system and manage the risks on its balance sheet effectively.
3. Discharge the Bank's enhanced role for financial stability.
4. Enhance the Bank's surveillance capacity to gather and analyse intelligence from external sources in order to support its policy objectives.
5. Influence the design and functioning of the international monetary and financial framework.
6. Reinforce public confidence in the Bank's role in the monetary and financial stability framework through a focused communication strategy.
7. Deliver efficient and effective notes issuance, banking and payments services.
8. Ensure the Bank has the organisational capacity and the right people and skills to carry out its strategic priorities.

Only 40 years ago the clearing banks held around 30 percent of their assets in short-term liquid instruments. In March 2009 that liquid assets ratio was down to about 1 percent. Only ten years ago the major UK banks made virtually no recourse to short-term funding in wholesale markets either at home or abroad. Now in March 2009 some 25 percent of customer loans were funded by such short-term borrowing in wholesale markets. In other words, not only did the UK banks fail to maintain an adequate liquidity reserve, but they took into their asset portfolios short-term assets carrying very high risk and complex structures which could not be easily unravelled. This was in no way sensible. HBoS and RBS found they had no alternative as this source of funding abruptly dried up and they had to agree to nationalisation. Meanwhile every single one of the hitherto rock-steady building societies that de-mutualised in the 1980s and 1990s and that abandoned the traditional well-tried statutory constraints of their deposit base have succumbed to merger or takeover. Not a single one has survived as an independent entity. This is a profoundly sad story for all those UK house-owners and small businessmen who found their hard-earned savings in jeopardy and the cost of replacement finance rising beyond their reach.

Giving the world a lead

Leslie O'Brien, 1971

This was the year when the Bretton Woods system finally broke down. It did this, not in dishonour, but because after a quarter of a century the world has greatly changed, and makeshift expedients were no longer acceptable. It must give great satisfaction to us all that as we come to the end of one era and prepare for the next, the UK is strong again and has not been backward in giving the world a lead.

Remarks by the Governor at the dinner given by the Lord Mayor to the Bankers and Merchants of the City of London on 21 October 1971.

The First Inflation Target

Norman Lamont

Chancellor of the Exchequer 1990–93, speaking to the Threadneedle Club on 20 October 2008

When I was Chancellor, I introduced an inflation target for the Bank of England for the first time. This was the new framework for monetary policy following the breakdown of the Exchange Rate Mechanism (ERM).

For the best part of the 1990s and the early part of this decade, this regime appeared to work remarkably well. However, the Labour Government moved to a narrower definition of inflation which excluded housing and also removed the requirement which I inserted to pay attention to broad money. This meant interest rates were lower than they should have been.

It seems to me that the whole regime of inflation targeting needs to be rethought alongside wider considerations of financial stability.

PART TWO

Monetary Policy Fundamentals

The prime objective of the Bank of England (and most other central banks) today is to ensure an agreed level of price stability through the nation by the flexible and prudent management of monetary policy. This function is rarely performed by other agencies. It is no easy task. Today the Monetary Policy Committee in the Bank of England, established in 1997, works to a Government guideline (2 percent per annum in January 2011), and for over a decade has been remarkably successful in adhering to this level and producing a firm base for economic growth at a level markedly higher than that of other members of the European Union. More recently, UK inflation has risen above the target level and the Bank has had much more difficulty in holding inflation down and mitigating the effects of worldwide recession.

Nonetheless the development of the continuous analysis of the key indicators necessary to guide monetary policy has attracted worldwide attention to the UK and the Bank of England procedures have become for many other central banks the preferred mechanism of choice. As a result the Bank of England Centre for Central Banking Studies (CCBS) runs seminars in London for some 1,500 participants a year drawn from over 100 central banks and, in 2007 for example, ran seminars and regional workshops in 25 countries overseas. The Bank is also heavily involved in providing input to similar meetings organised by the Bank for International Settlements, the European Central Bank, the International Monetary Fund, the Asian Development Bank, the Bank of Japan and the People's Bank of China.

Achieving Price Stability

Achieving domestic price stability is, however, no easy matter, given the turmoil in exchange markets and high volatility in the commodity and stock markets engendered by the failures in the banking system in 2007-9 and the consequent loss of confidence and fears worldwide that global economic growth might fail to be sustained in the decade ahead at the rates achieved over the previous three decades.

Domestic price stability depends also on external management – the preservation of long-term stability in the exchange markets and the long-term health of the banks and other sectors of the financial system. Globalisation of these systems means that major events anywhere in the world, transmitted instantly, can have huge and often unforeseen effects on the financial and exchange markets. For the UK, these factors are particularly important with one-third of global transactions in foreign exchange being handled through London and the UK financial sector employing just short of a million people. The banking and liquidity crisis of 2008-9, part imported from the United States, therefore produced acute pressures on the UK banks and the UK economy requiring extraordinary measures to keep the financial and economic show on the road.

The Instruments of Monetary Policy

Money responds, similar to any commodity or manufactured good or service, to the fundamental laws of supply and demand. Too much money and credit engenders over-heating, inflation and too much high-risk investment. Too little can quickly generate a credit famine and acute hardship for small- and medium-sized businesses and householders unable to obtain or service their house-mortgage commitments. The aim of the Governor or President of a central bank is always to keep the economic ship-of-state firmly and safely in the deep-water channel without fear of grounding or shipwreck whatever the confused congestion of distressed vessels around him or any extreme bad weather coming in from overseas.

A central bank has two fundamental means of implementing monetary policy. It can influence the *price* of money by setting interest-rates or it can affect the *volume* of money by 'quantitative lending' – pumping money into the economy through the banks on terms which empower the central bank and/or government to take it back again whenever they deem that necessary.

Over the last three years, the Bank's hold on interest rates has been weakened by being trapped by very low rates (down to 0.5 percent). That is why the Bank has had to resort to unprecedented levels of 'quantitative easing' over the last three years. Yet the Bank has other useful arrows within its monetary policy sheaf. It can use its own balance sheet to target and impact developments in particular markets with the knowledge that these are only short-term strategies which have often been highly successful over the past 300 or so years. From time to time over this period, it has, as in 2007-9, had to intervene and take over failed banks and again over its long history, it has achieved remarkable success and averted economic collapse and wider financial catastrophe.

Within only a few months in 2008–9 the Federal Reserve was obliged to increase its balance sheet four-fold with little warning and on a staggering scale – from about $800 billion to well over $3 trillion. The Bank of England was inevitably sucked into a similar process, choosing to use an Asset Purchase facility of £75 billion which, between May and November 2009 was increased to £200 billion, in order to pump desperately needed liquidity into the system. Bankers and governments all over the world were perplexed by the speed and scale of these reactions.

Central Bank Credibility

Paul Tucker, now a Deputy Governor of the Bank, put the policy fundamentals very clearly in an article published in the Bank of England Quarterly Bulletin of July 2006, giving clear warning of troubles ahead. Maintaining and reinforcing central bank credibility cannot to be taken for granted, he said: 'it needs to be earned and re-earned, over and over again'.

This involves defining clearly the national interest, free of government tinkering, media speculation, market rumour or the undue pressure of the banks and industrial leaders. He lists the main components of that credibility as:

- Being very publicly committed to anchoring medium-term inflation expectations in line with a clear target.
- Ensuring that inflation outturns are, on average, in line with the target.
- Being seen to be committed to the essentially technical job of professional analysis of current commercial and economic conditions and the underlying structure of the economy.
- Being ready to do whatever is necessary to maintain well-anchored inflation expectations.

Another aspect of central bank credibility is the strength of its intelligence in the financial sector acquired by being constantly out-and-about in the financial sector and industry and knowing the key personalities well. Traditionally, the Bank of England has been very good at this, but this three-century old, well-proven process was badly damaged by the abrupt transfer of regulatory powers to the Financial

Services Authority established in 1997 (and may now be remedied by the decision in 2010 to restore overall control to the Bank of England). The concern of the Bank focussed not on the establishment of another institution to share the workload, but on the lack of clarity on how danger signals identified by the FSA could be promptly transmitted to the Bank and whether the Bank might be unable to act swiftly and discreetly in its traditional style without up-to-date evidence to hand. The precious baby of discretion and deterrence had been thrown out with the bathwater, the golden calf of traditional central banking buried under a mound of useless paper.

Coping with the Crisis

By the fourth quarter of 2009, UK growth had become negative: GDP was 3.1 percent less than a year earlier. Unemployment, as measured by the Labour Force Survey had risen steeply to 7.8 percent of the workforce. This was clear evidence of the impact of the financial crisis and of serious danger to the UK economy as a whole. Yet the Bank of England stuck to its guns and weathered the storm. By early 2010 advance indicators were predicting a return to a modest level of economic growth within the year. The impact on the sterling exchange rate had not been as precipitous as feared. A collapse of the banking system caused by the failure of several leading banks had been averted. This represents a major achievement on a scale far beyond anything experienced in the UK over the past 317 years of the Bank's history

The Bank has, since summer 2009, embarked on a deepening of market contact and strengthened its presence in the City and real economy using its 12 regional agents and their staff (see Annex 5). Within nine months, the nine members of the Monetary Policy Committee (see Annex 4) also travelled extensively within the UK giving a total of 32 formal published speeches and undertaking a total of 56 visits outside Greater London while the Governor and senior staff attended a total of 14 parliamentary hearings and 10 hearings of the Treasury Committee of the House of Commons. Far more efficient and effective than ever before, the MPC system is also as transparent as it could be. The monthly *MPC Inflation Report* and minutes of all MPC meetings are made available and explained and discussed with the media. Two Monetary Policy Roundtable Conferences are held each year – participants include economists from a wide range of private sector companies and institutions as well as representatives of public sector bodies and invited university professors and other academic specialists in this field.

In three talks to the Threadneedle Club in 1994, 1998 and 2004, the late Eddie George (Governor 1993–2003) outlined the key current issues regarding monetary policy. Mervyn King, the then Deputy Governor addressed the Club on the same topic in 2002, only a very short time before the announcement of his appointment as Governor. Over the last five years the Club has also been addressed on the subject by three former Chancellors of the Exchequer, Nigel Lawson in 2006, Norman Lamont in 2008 and in October 2010 by Geoffrey Howe, when the Chairman of Morgan Stanley International, Sir David Walker, was the lead speaker.

"Central Banking is not explained by giving reasons.
What I rely on is feelings."

Montagu Norman, Governor 1920–44

PART THREE

The Exchange Rate and Externals

No monetary policy can be conducted without a close eye on the exchange rate and the level of official foreign exchange reserves available to intervene if a country's exchange rate is considered too high or too low. In the case of the United Kingdom, this had been frequently a, if not the, prime concern of the Bank of England in keeping the export of UK goods and services highly competitive in world markets. Equally, high UK dependence on imported food, raw materials, energy and manufactures placed, and still places, a high cost and persistent strain on the UK balance of payments. A too strong sterling exchange rate means we can import cheaply but export with difficulty; a weakened exchange rate poses questions for the ability to import enough food, oil and other necessary imports. In the 1970s new domestic supplies of natural gas began to diminish the demand for imported oil and from 1980 when the UK achieved self-sufficiency in oil consumption, these pressures on the UK balance of payments were greatly alleviated. Today, the UK has slipped back into high and rising dependency on imported oil, gas and coal and the future costs of oil, gas and coal are already beginning to feature prominently again in the formulation of UK economic policy.

Imbalances on Current Account

John Maynard Keynes
speaking at the Bretton Woods Conference in 1944

'The process of adjustment is compulsory for the debtor and voluntary for the creditor. If the creditor does not choose to make, or allow, his share of the adjustment, he suffers no inconvenience. For whilst a country's reserve cannot fall below zero, there is no ceiling which sets an upper limit.'

One of the main causes of the recent crisis of 2007–9 did in fact relate to fluctuations in the value of the US dollar and the pound sterling. Its origin was in the United States and it spread rapidly to the UK with consequences which severely affected the rest of the world.

By 2007 both the USA and UK had developed over a long period of time large and growing imbalances on their current account. Inflows of capital into these economies from outside became so large that they lowered market interest rates to levels much lower than they would otherwise have been. The US and UK banks had thus been deprived of what they considered a normal level of earnings to preserve profitability and a balanced portfolio. As Mervyn King put it, the banks felt that they had to keep on dancing while the music was playing. So they began to explore alternative ways of improving yields on the funds they held by increasing leverage, taking on more risk and making that risk much less transparent. In both the USA and, to a lesser extent, in the UK, the banks relaxed their lending conditions to attract more business, fuelling, for example, the real-estate boom and attracting large volumes of funds from outside to the housing and other property markets. Speculation fed on these inflated expectations and was transferred to the commodity markets until inevitably the bubble burst.

A Self-balancing System (in Theory!)

In theory, the world financial system is self-balancing over time. Countries with rising external deficits soon find that their credit-rating is adversely affected and they are obliged to rein in their external expenditure as their exchange rate begins to weaken. Major international banks are the first to feel these impacts and, in these circumstances, should begin to exert stricter lending conditions and to place caps on the level of borrowing of those countries that are the worst offenders. In the worst cases the IMF steps in to provide temporary finance on the strict condition that each maverick government will take the appropriate recommended action at home to cool its overheated domestic economy.

For the rest of the industrialised world and most of the developing world, matters did not appear too serious. They were able to achieve price stability on their own with steady rates of growth. What was happening in the USA and UK was largely of little interest and beyond their ken.

The consequences of the US and UK banks blithely pursuing micro-objectives to boost their profitability, while the imbalances of both the UK and USA were growing exponentially were devastating – a sudden collapse of confidence in Wall Street and the City of London bringing a severe global downturn affecting virtually every country in the world. Once imbalances on the scale of those of the USA and UK were appreciated, the counterpart surplus countries led by China and Japan saw severe impacts on their exports and an acute slow-down in industrial production and a drying up of their export markets that looked as if it might persist for several years and possibly decades. Other countries that had relied on a steadily rising level of borrowing overseas rapidly found that this option was quickly vanishing.

Loud pleas from the USA and UK about the need for symmetry in the responses of both debtor and surplus countries fell largely on deaf ears as it was very hard for the very large number of small- and medium-sized surplus countries to see how their own modest contributions, involving in each state considerable pain and disappointment of public expectations, could be made to add up to an effective global counterweight to the massive size of the problem in the USA and UK.

It is now widely agreed that the G20 countries have to give the lead in three directions:

- A collective commitment by all members of the G20 to restore confidence.
- In each country where the banking system has failed, there must be an immediate promise to restructure and recapitalise the banks, so that they can resume their normal functions and support the renewed flow of credit to their own and other economies. Strong regional co-ordination will be needed to achieve this.
- A model is needed worldwide to provide exit strategies to unwind all the unprecedented official policy actions which, with very high levels of debt, threaten to place a long-term brake on economic growth, social welfare and the future rapid response of the international finance and commodity markets.

The problem is still with us. It has in fact been developing for well over a decade. The entry of the Asian 'tigers' into the global trading and financial systems had prepared the way and the massive arrival of China into their ranks had built up huge new pools of savings, much of which were channelled into foreign financial assets. For the industrialised countries, all focussed on maintaining levels of output and employment under a stable level of inflation, these inflows came as a godsend bringing downward pressure on interest rates and inflation.

For the holders of these foreign financial assets in the US and UK, the main aim was to find assets offering a higher rate of return with (apparently) lower risk than could be found elsewhere. Higher returns could only be generated by taking higher risks. As a result money was lent on much easier terms. This helped to push up asset prices as interest rates were falling.

An Unsustainable Outcome

From the early 1990s to the start of the crisis in 2007, total debt in the UK relative to Gross Domestic Product almost doubled. Only about one-third of this increase in total debt went to the real economy. The rest was accounted for by lending to the financial sector. The Bank of England spotted the danger and signalled repeatedly in speeches by the Governor and detailed analysis in the *Quarterly Bulletin* that these developments on this scale were unsustainable. As far as the Government was concerned, the economy seemed to be doing well and regulatory reform had been vested firmly in the hands of their own new public-sector institution, the Financial Services Authority. The Bank's advice fell on very deaf ears.

Although much remains to be done, there are some chinks of light coming through. In the last quarter of 2008 through the peak of the panic worldwide, output fell by 3 percent in the USA and UK, by 6 percent in Germany and by 7 percent in Japan. In 2008 employment in the USA fell by over 5 million, in the euro area by almost 2 million and in the UK by half a million. These are serious numbers which have not been repeated on the same scale in 2009 or 2010.

As far as the Bank of England is concerned, standing firm in adversity and surveying the considerable damage inflicted on the economy, it is clear that a turning-point has been reached and that the seeds of recovery are already sprouting. The focus has to be on ensuring that such dreadful events cannot happen again.

One Brick on Top of Another

Mervyn King
Speaking at the University of Exeter on
19 January 2010

The reason continuing large deficits are not sustainable indefinitely is that for every current account deficit there is an equal net capital flow in the opposite direction. Even if those flows remain constant in size, they imply an ever increasing stock of international asset and liability positions. Today China alone has reserves of over two trillion dollars, and Japan another trillion dollars. Adding inexorably to the stock of international assets and liabilities is like adding one brick on top of another to form a tower. With skill, it can be done for a surprisingly long time. But eventually the moment comes when adding one more brick causes the tower to fall down. If countries do not work together to reduce the 'too high to last' imbalances, a crisis of one sort or another in financial markets is only too likely.

PART FOUR

The Health of the Financial Sector

Financial Stability

For over three centuries, the Bank of England has, without statutory mandate, performed the principal role as the guardian of financial stability within the United Kingdom. It has been ready to intervene on behalf of the nation in liquidity and foreign exchange crises and it has been repeatedly involved in sorting out major banks and other financial institutions whenever they have run into serious trouble.

What is meant by financial stability? Until quite recently there has been no precise definition. Generally, it assumes that the key financial institutions are stable and, by prudent management, are able to meet all their contractual obligations without interruption or outside assistance. Transactions between the key players can therefore be undertaken confidently at prices which do not vary substantially over short periods. It is this stability of the banks and other players that underpins the well-being of the economy by providing stability in the value of money and credit, together with reassurance that the risks of high inflation or abrupt deflation are low. This, hopefully, should provide a strong basis and incentive for investment and economic growth as well as for the optimum utilisation of the labour, skills and enterprise available in the economy.

Sermons and Burials Only

Following the emergence of problems in Northern Rock in 2007, the Labour Government drafted resolutions to define financial stability more closely. Senior Bank officials were quick to point out that, without a new tool to deliver such stability, a statutory financial stability provision was unlikely to change the way the Bank operates in practice.

Mervyn King chose the Lord Mayor's Banquet on 17 June 2009, one week after the first meeting of the Financial Stability Committee set up under the Banking Act 2009 to make the point again in public, adding a most subtle but relevant reference to the bank mergers then under discussion:

'The Bank of England has a new statutory responsibility for financial stability. Bank Rate is the instrument we employ to achieve monetary stability, and should be used exclusively for that purpose.

To achieve financial stability the powers of the Bank are limited to those of voice and the new resolution powers. The Bank finds itself in the position rather like that of a church whose congregation attends weddings and burials, but ignores the sermons in between. Like the church, we cannot promise that bad things won't happen to our flock – the prevention of all financial crises is in neither our nor anyone else's power, as a study of history or human nature would reveal. And experience suggests that attempts to encourage a better life through the power of the voice is not enough. Warnings are unlikely to be effective when people are being asked to change behaviour which seems to them highly profitable. So it is not entirely clear how the Bank will be able to discharge its new statutory responsibility if we can do no more than issue sermons or organise burials.'

Understanding what the Governor of the Bank of England is really saying in public requires a practised ear and a keen eye for the body language. Over the last three centuries, it is not merely what the Governor says that matters. Much more important is what he does not say. So an experienced financial journalist covering a major event such as the annual Lord Mayor's Dinner might be well advised to go along with a detailed list of what he expects to hear, ticking off each item as it comes up. From the missing items he will concoct his story, which on the text of the speech above might begin with a clearly indicated warning from the Governor (deliberately omitted from the text), which might be paraphrased:

'I imagine you have been expecting me to comment on the rumours traded all over the City over the past few days about various proposed mergers of leading financial institutions. But you know very well that we are deeply involved in such events at the Bank and that I cannot comment on them. Nor can we promise that good things will happen to our flock. Indeed, on the one hand, some very bad things might happen to some of them, while, on the other hand, we may witness, but cannot anticipate, some joyful couplings bringing affluence and an abundance of offspring. Meanwhile, despite the new instructions from the Government, we will have to go on doing what we did before. So I will restrict my remarks to issuing sermons and organising burials.'

Redefining the Bank's Financial Stability Mission

In May 2010 the Court endorsed a new declaration of the Bank's two core purposes:

1. *Monetary Stability*
'Monetary stability means stable prices and confidence in the currency. Stable prices are defined by the Government's inflation target, which the Bank seeks to meet through the decisions delegated to the Monetary Policy Committee, explaining those decisions transparently and implementing them effectively in the money markets.'

2. *Financial Stability*
'Financial stability entails detecting and reducing threats to

the financial system as a whole. Such threats are detected through the Bank's surveillance and market intelligence functions. They are reduced by strengthening infrastructure, and by financial and other operations, at home and abroad, including in exceptional circumstances, by acting as the lender of last resort.'

Following the recent decision announced by the new Conservative-Liberal Coalition Government to wind up the Financial Services Authority, progress is being made to divide its functions between the Prudential Regulation Authority (PRA) constituted as a new division of the Bank of England and led by a new Deputy Governor covering 2,000 banks and other lead financial institutions in the City and the Consumer Protection and Markets Authority (CPMA) covering 99,000 firms regulated hitherto by the Office of Fair Trading.

A detailed strategy for the Bank's financial stability mission was approved by the Court in December 2009 and incorporated in the Bank's Priorities in 2010–11 published in the Annual Report for 2010. This is now being revised and updated to take account of these latest developments.

From the Governor's Speech to the CBI on 12 November 1996

'aiming for permanent price stability'

Inflation is essentially a symptom of an emerging imbalance between demand and supply in the economy. We have learned that you cannot secure economic growth in anything other than the short-term simply by pumping up demand without regard to the underlying capacity to meet it. So what we are really trying to do by aiming for permanent price stability is to achieve lasting **economic** stability in a much broader sense – a sustainable balance between demand and supply growth.

Eddie George

PART FIVE

The Fiction of False Expectations
The Myth of Impregnability
Discretion, Secrecy and Continuity

Trapped within a High Wall

Fiction is fiction, but, from time to time and here and there, the general public's belief in fiction is a fact. This is a real problem for the Bank of England trapped on its island site behind its ancient, and still today formidable, defensive wall. It appears impregnable and everlasting. The truth is, of course, very different. The Bank of England today is not invincible. It could be marginalised by any government adopting a policy of asserting direct control, down-sizing the staff and outsourcing or privatising most of its day-to-day functions and activities. It could be swallowed up almost overnight to become a mere outpost of the European Central Bank. It could lose its identity and character by focussing on the short-term and failing to recruit and train and equip itself for the long-term. Yet the general public is unaware of such dangers and largely ignorant of what goes on behind the wall.

True, there are many accounts of the work of the Bank scattered over the last 300 or so years. Some are by biographers, some by staff and directors, only one or two by Governors (often using hired journalists), and many by academics. None of these, however have had much impact on the population at large. So they turn for a stereotype to fiction.

For novelists, travel- and crime-writers and many others, the Old Lady provides a particular fascination. For a start, the Bank of England is well known to their readers, leaping out day-by-day at anyone whenever they take a Bank of England banknote from their pocket or purse. It is the acknowledged centre of the City of London, a prominent temple of rectitude planted, so it appears among a teeming City of London multitude driven by Mammon. It is at the principal crossroads of the City and the hub of another major intersection of underground lines beneath its feet with a bullion treasure beyond belief. Unrivalled intelligence tentacles stretch through trade, inter-governmental cooperation and capital investment to the ends of the earth. This archetypal global octopus offers to the imaginative mind, mystery, secrets, strange adventures in foreign lands and a deep 300-year old acquaintance with crime, particularly treason, spying, theft, fraud and forgery and all the weaker aspects of human nature including greed, addiction, blackmail, extortion and murder. Where better to begin or set one's mystery or love story or adventure or intrigue or part of it in such an unconventional setting?

The Assumption of Permanence

Add to this the Old Lady's traditional reticence and distrust of the media and her inexplicable silences (some of which have been known to extend for as much as a hundred years). We have to turn to fiction as a clue to what the general public thinks of the Bank and its future. And, of course, that widely-read popular fiction, prone to endemic exaggeration, together with a steady stream of spy-films, television docu-dramas and inquisitive television soaps reinforces the popular fascination with hidden power, commercial conspiracy and political leverage as well as, quite simply, with questionable individuals misusing their and other people's money – gold, silver, copper, banknotes, bonds, bank-balances, real-estate and other assets. No wonder the activity of the Bank has to be encased in secrecy, in private codes and in much red tape. In terms of public relations, it has, over three centuries, become the victim of its own discretion and prudence.

The Lure of Money and Gold

As an illustration of my points about the myth of permanence and the perennial public interest in vast quantities of gold and banknotes and the like, I have selected extracts from four very different authors stretching over a century and a half. Here, Charles Dickens was interested primarily in the bank staff and their eccentricities. Jules Verne was fascinated by the worldwide use of the pound sterling. All his hero had to do to spend the best part of three months travelling round the world with his servant for free was to place £20,000 in Bank of England notes in a carpet-bag and agree a high-risk wager with five friends for £4,000 each. Then follows a predictable French tirade on the lax security in the Bank of England – unthinkable in the closely ordered world of the Banque de France. Ian Fleming describes the first visit of James Bond to the Bank as having 'the heavy, grave atmosphere of immense wealth' and permits him to listen to a lecture on why gold is so different from any other commodity on earth. Rupert Pennant-Rea contrasts the solemn, polite welcome of the pink-coated messengers on the lead character's arrival in the Main Entrance Hall with the sudden realisation that his final departure might be no more than a few hours away.

Charles Dickens

First Charles Dickens describing a visit to the Bank of England in *The Pickwick Papers*, first published in April 1836. The group consisted of Tony Weller, Sam Weller, two fat coachmen, Mr Solomon Pell, their lawyer and Mr Wilkins Flasher of the Stock Exchange. They were visiting Consols Office for Weller Senior, executor of the late second Mrs Weller to examine the level of her holding of what Mr Weller refers to as 'four and a half per cent counsels' and were astonished to find all the clerks hungrily eating sandwiches.

The Bank of England Sandwich

Wilkins Flasher, Esquire, now condescended to receive Mr Solomon Pell's instructions, and having filled up some printed forms, requested the party to follow him to the Bank: which they did; Mr Weller and his three friends staring at all they beheld in unbounded astonishment, and Sam encountering everything with a coolness nothing could disturb.

Crossing a court-yard which was all noise and bustle; and passing a couple of porters who seemed dressed to match the red fire engine which was wheeled away into a corner; they passed into an office where their business was to be transacted, where Mr Pell and Mr Flasher left them standing for a few moments, while they went upstairs into the Will Office.

'Wot place is this here?' whispered the mottle-faced gentleman to the elder Mr Weller.

'What are them gen'l'men a settin' behind the counters?' asked the hoarse coachman.

'Reduced counsels, I s'pose,' replied Mr Weller. 'Ain't they the reduced counsels, Samivel?'

'Wy, yiu don't suppose the reduced counsels is alive, do you?' inquired Sam, with some disdain.

'How should I know?' retorted Mr Weller; 'I thought they looked wery like it. Wot are they then?'

'Clerks,' replied Sam.

' Wot are they all eatin' ham sangwidges for?' inquired his father.

"Cos it's in their dooty, I suppose,' replied Sam, 'It's a part o' the system; they're a doin'it here all day long!'

Jules Verne

Second, Jules Verne who published *Le Tour du Monde en Quatre-Vingt Jours* in Paris in 1873. Since then it has been in print continuously in several languages.

Around the World for Free With Bank of England Notes

Phileas Fogg paid for his round-the-world trip by putting £20,000 in Bank of England notes in a carpet-bag carried by his servant Passepartout. He took no other notes or coin or cheque-book and incurred no debt. Not only an obsessive time-keeper but a meticulous accountant, he was also blessed with an ability to keep cool in the harshest of circumstances – truly the hallmark of the Bank of England official.

The same night, he pledged his remaining £20,000 to five bridge-playing friends in the Reform Club led by a Bank of England Director, Gauthier Ralph on a straight bet for £4,000 each that he could not complete the journey within 1,920 hours or 115,200 minutes.

It was Gauthier who confirmed to the group that a theft of £55,000 in Bank of England notes had taken place in the Bank only three days before Fogg's departure. The Metropolitan Police had quickly discovered that the prime suspect was a gentleman, and had already despatched several detectives, including one, Mr Fix to Suez. The description given matched that of Phileas Fogg closely.

Fix caught up with Fogg and Passepartout at Suez but all three moved on before the arrival of the arrest warrant. When Fogg discovered that his first-class railway tickets between Bombay and Calcutta included a stretch of 50 miles which had not yet been built, he bought an elephant for £2,000. Later, in mid-Atlantic, when the Captain refused to sail on to Liverpool, he purchased the entire steamship and proceeded to chop out all the wood in it to provide adequate fuel for the boiler. Imprisoned on arrival in Southampton, Fogg nonetheless managed to arrive in time at the Reform Club to claim and collect his £20,000 winnings and to learn that three days previously, precisely 80 days after the theft of the £55,000 in notes from the counter of the Bank of England, a suspect had been arrested and had made a full confession of guilt.

A Gentleman Thief at The Bank of England

Half an hour later several members of the Reform came in and drew up to the fire-place, where a coal fire was burning steadily. They were Mr Fogg's usual partners at whist: Andrew Stuart, an engineer; John Sullivan and Samuel Fallentin, bankers; Thomas Flanagan, a brewer; and Gauthier Ralph, one of the directors of the Bank of England. All were rich and highly respectable, even in a club which counts among its members the princes of English trade and finance.

'Well, Ralph,' said Thomas Flanagan, 'what about that robbery?'

...'The Daily Telegraph *says that he is a gentleman.'*

It was Phileas Fogg, whose head now emerged from behind his newspapers, who made this remark. He bowed to his friends, and entered into the conversation. The affair which formed its subject, and which was the talk of the town, had occurred three days before at the Bank of England. A package of bank notes, to the value of fifty-five thousand pounds, had been taken from the table of the principal cashier who had been engaged in registering the receipt of three shillings and sixpence. Of course he could not have his eyes everywhere.

Let it be known that the Bank of England shows a touching confidence in the honesty of the public. There are neither guards nor gratings to protect its treasures and gold, silver and bank notes are freely exposed, at the mercy of the first comer. A keen observer of English customs relates that, being in one of the rooms of the Bank one day, he had the curiosity to examine a gold ingot weighing some seven or eight pounds. He took it up, scrutinised it, passed it to his neighbour, he to the next man, and so on until the ingot, going from hand to hand, was transferred to the end of a dark entry. It did not return to its place for half an hour. Meanwhile, the cashier had not so much as raised his head. But in the present instance things had not gone so smoothly.

The package of notes not being found when five o'clock sounded from the ponderous clock in the 'drawing office', the amount was passed to profit and loss. As soon as the robbery was discovered, select detectives hastened off to Liverpool, Glasgow, Le Havre, Suez, Brindisi, New York and other ports, inspired by the promise of a reward of two thousand pounds and five per cent on the amount that might be recovered. Detectives were also charged with narrowly watching those who arrived or left London by rail, and a judicial examination was at once entered upon.

There were real grounds for supposing, as The Daily Telegraph *said, that the thief did not belong to a professional band. On the day of the robbery a well-dressed gentleman of polished manners, and with a well-to-do air, had been observed going to and fro in the paying room, where the crime was committed. A description of him was easily procured and sent to the detectives; and some good minds, of whom Ralph was one, hoped that the thief would not escape. The papers and clubs were full of the affair, and everywhere people were discussing the probabilities of a successful pursuit. The Reform Club was particularly agitated, one of its members being a Bank official.*

Ian Fleming

Ian Fleming was born in 1908 and educated at Eton and Sandhurst. For a short time, he worked as a journalist with Reuters and elsewhere in the City before joining the Foreign Office. During World War II, he served in British Naval Intelligence and in the aftermath, he was appointed Foreign Manager at *The Sunday Times*. *Casino Royale*, the first of his James Bond 007 thrillers was published in 1953,

Moonraker in 1955, *Diamonds are Forever* in 1956, *From Russia With Love* in 1957 and *Goldfinger* two years later. His own suave, charming, decisive personality, his passion for guns and gadgets of all kinds and for very fast cars, gambling and short-lived romance matched quite well the character of his hero. He died of heart failure in 1964 at the age of 56.

The Heavy, Grave Atmosphere of Immense Riches

'Bond walked up the steps and through the fine bronze portals and into the spacious, softly echoing entrance hall of the Bank of England and looked around him. Under his feet glittered the brilliant gold patterns of the Boris Anrep mosaics; beyond, through twenty-feet high arched windows, green grass and geraniums blazed in the central courtyard. To right and left were spacious vistas of polished Hopton Wood stone. Over all hung the neutral smell of air-conditioned air and the heavy, grave atmosphere of immense riches.'

The first words of *Goldfinger*, Chapter Six – Talk of Gold

The Great Thing to Remember About Gold

'Aha, yes – well now, the great thing to remember about gold is that it's the most valuable and most easily marketable commodity in the world. You can go to any town in the world, almost to any village, and hand over a piece of gold and get goods and services in exchange. Right?' Colonel Smithers's voice had taken on a new briskness. His eyes were alight. He had his lecture pat. Bond sat back. He was prepared to listen to anyone who was master of his subject, any subject. 'And the next thing to remember,' Colonel Smithers held up his pipe in warning, 'is that gold is virtually untraceable. Sovereigns have no serial numbers. If gold bars have Mint marks stamped on them the marks can be shaved off or the bar can be melted down and made into a new bar. That makes it almost impossible to check on the whereabouts of gold, or its origins, or its movements round the world. In England, for instance, we at the Bank

can only count the gold in our own vaults, in the vaults of other banks and at the Mint, and make a rough guess at the amounts held by the jewellery trade and the pawnbroking fraternity.'

'Why are you so anxious to know how much gold there is in England?'

'Because gold and currencies backed by gold are the foundation of our international credit. We can only tell what the true strength of the pound is, and other countries can only tell it, by knowing the amount of valuta we have behind our currency. And my main job, Mr Bond –' Colonel Smithers' bland eyes had become exceptionally sharp – 'is to watch for any leakage of gold out of England – out of anywhere in the sterling area. And when I spot a leakage, an escape of gold towards some country where it can be exchanged more profitably than at the buying price, it is my job to put the CID Gold Squad on to the fugitive gold and try to get it back into our vaults, plug the leak and arrest the people responsible. And the trouble is, Mr Bond –' Colonel Smithers gave a forlorn shrug of the shoulders – 'that gold attracts the biggest, the most ingenious criminals. They are very hard, very hard indeed, to catch.'

Rupert Pennant-Rea

Rupert Lascelles Pennant-Rea was born and brought up in Rhodesia. He studied economics at Trinity College, Dublin and the University of Manchester. He worked at the Bank of England from 1973 to 1977 before moving to *The Economist* and being appointed Editor (1986-93) and then returned to the Old Lady as Deputy Governor (1993-5).

Gold Foil, published in 1978, is set in the 1980s – some few years after the publication date. It tells a fictitious tale embellished with many accurately described locations and rituals in and out of the Bank. The world's central banks, meeting behind closed doors at the Bank for International Settlements in Basle, agree that only a return to some form of gold standard can rescue the Western democracies from the insanity of hyper-inflation caused by excessive government spending. Simultaneously, the Russian Government is meeting in the Kremlin to decide how Russia, faced with falling supplies of its own gold and collapsing foreign currency reserves and costly rising dissidence throughout the Soviet Union, can finance its purchases of grain and vital commodities and new technology from the West.

Suddenly the viewpoint of the South African government, by far the world's largest supplier of gold, becomes of paramount importance. But the problem for the Western bankers is to decide whether, with widespread civil unrest in South Africa, they should be dealing with the white government in Pretoria or the two principal exiled political parties in London.

The Governor of the Bank, who bears an uncanny resemblance to Gordon Richardson (Governor 1973-83), later Lord Richardson of Duntisbourne, follows the Bank's traditional style in such matters. He decides to send a young high-flyer, James Glendinning, on a discreet fact-finding mission to Pretoria and Johannesburg for a secret meeting with the Head of the Gold Department of the South African Reserve Bank.

Hard on the heels of James Glendinning, unfortunately, follows one Caroline Manning, a bright, beautiful, radical, seductive and uninhibited New York journalist, intent on securing 'one of the greatest journalistic scoops of all time' – at whatever cost. James duly succumbs on page 100 to her scent and her Indian silk and to her lips ('very warm and soft'). Their passionate coupling (in Room 215 of his Johannesburg hotel) , is abruptly discontinued by the sort of excuse that only a well-trained Bank of England man could deliver convincingly in such circumstances – 'It's only my blasted sunburn'. It is too late. Glendinning lives on (through another 120 pages,) to see finally the error of his ways.

Between Civilisation and the Jungle

As he walked through the large doors of the Bank he acknowledged the respectful nods from the pink-coated doorkeepers. Occasionally, he wondered whether they really knew who he was – perhaps they nodded like that to everyone. He passed through the massive front hall with its marble pillars and intricately designed stone floors and turned left down a corridor to the Chief Cashier's office. It was all so familiar, and yet just as imposing as on the day he arrived as a nervous undergraduate for his interview.

He walked past some more pink coats: in a film recently made by the Bank, they had been described as looking as safe as the Bank of England. James had found himself murmuring in agreement until the awfulness of the cliché had struck him. In the American Federal Reserve, he always told his visitors, the attendants wore guns on their hips; but in the Bank it was only pink coats. He found this very reassuring – the difference between civilisation and the jungle. Whenever the pound slipped lower against the dollar, the pink coats were a comfort.

Extract from *Gold Foil,* Chapter 4

The First Whiff of Scandal

The loudspeaker was booming again, and James gratefully seized at an excuse to stop reading. The luggage was still delayed: the baggage handlers were apparently picketing the two Concordes, but British Airways hoped the matter would be resolved very shortly. In the meantime they apologised for the inconvenience.

But James Glendinning was very thankful for the inconvenience. He would have picketed the Concordes himself if that would have suspended time and reality a little longer. Outside this room, he could imagine the kind of reality that would be building up. In the Bank, the first whiff of scandal would send the staff into discreet huddles, and by the end of the day the place would be stiff with rumours. But what about the parlours? The Governor would immediately call in the Directors and the Chief, no doubt of that. Probably, he, James, would be asked in as well. Then there would be a telephone call from the Chancellor, maybe even from the Prime Minister. How much did they know – how much had the Governor told them? Perhaps the Governor would be compelled to resign...

James shuddered at this ultimate horror, and tried a different tack. What would be going on in Washington? The IMF, and Richter himself, would be seriously embarrassed. Did they know about the American intervention? The whole nightmare increasingly resembled an intricate web, but had it been spun by any one person? Or was it all a series of coincidences? 'Will you walk into my parlour...?' Well, he'd been caught in the web, and would shortly be eaten alive. He'd have to leave the Bank, his career in ruins ...'

Extract from *Gold Foil,* Chapter 31.

So, in summary, what are the features about the Bank of England that leap out from the above examples of English fiction? I would put eight of them, in descending order, all, in today's world, highly dubious:

1. An assumption of permanence and rock-like stability.
2. A fascination with immense quantities of gold and unlimited billions of paper money.
3. A strong interest in secrecy, total discretion and swift, subtle responses.
4. A dim awareness of huge global influence and power
5. A conviction that there is always a large reserve of first-class skills on tap.
6. A belief that the Bank always knows what is going on in the City.
7. A hunch that the Bank's independence from government might be good for all of us .
8. A hint that the traditional hallmark of a Bank of England official – keeping cool and polite, whatever the crisis or upheaval – might still be of value today.

The truth in the Old Lady is, of course, much stranger than fiction. In an elderly institution like the Bank of England, it is a surprise to discover, as in my time there, that there is nothing unusual in popping off to New York or Washington DC for the day on Concorde or, as in 1968, sending the Governor off to Canberra and back for a visit of 24 hours or to Hong Kong in 1993 for an even quicker turn-round, or as described in Chapter Ten, sending someone for two years to Washington DC at no more than two weeks' notice, accompanied on the *Queen Mary* by his favourite books and magazines, his 7-month pregnant wife and his dogs.

To a member of the public straying for some special reason deep inside, the Bank might seem a curious fictional wonderland, out of time and place, at the bottom of a deep, deep hole. They might show you in the floor mosaics the double-headed portrait of Governor Norman who commissioned them or the alignments in the designs which, when projected to the other side of the Garden Court all meet at the same point under the Governor's chair. Or they will take you to the huge black pillars, to spot the fossils of marine crustaceans or, at the bottom of the deep hole, three floors down at the foot of the main staircase, an intact Roman tessellated pavement of immense beauty discovered on the site in the 1920s.

There is even a suggestion by Kenneth Grahame that Lewis Carroll found inspiration in the Bank of England. To Alice, falling down the rabbit-hole or passing through the looking glass meant everything was too big or too small or back-to-front – but the Queen, the Duchess, Tweedledum and Tweedledee, and the White Rabbit and the Caterpillar, and even the playing card servants would see it differently. For them, this was the all-encompassing reality. For them, locked up inside in their own little wonderland, as Kenneth Grahame drily observed, there was no other world.

Kenneth Grahame and The Wind in the Willows.
A 1908 Treatise on Central Banking

PART SIX

A 1908 Treatise on Central Banking

Paul Tempest

Kenneth Grahame, Secretary of the Bank of England 1898–1908

Kenneth Grahame was a most remarkable top official of the Bank of England, occupying one of the three posts created on its foundation in 1694. He was 39 on appointment, one of the youngest to hold any of those three posts in the 317-year history of the Bank. And he held the post for ten years with distinction through a most turbulent period in the Bank's history. Yet he left abruptly one afternoon in June 1908 and never returned. There is no doubt from contemporary accounts and his private papers now lodged in the Bodleian Library, Oxford that he was both angry and disappointed about his treatment in the Bank at this time, yet in the 24 years remaining until his death in 1932, he appears to have made no attempt to seek compensation or other legal redress or to criticise the Bank in any way. His letters to friends and family reflect an unwillingness to discuss the matter. All offers by leading publishers to commission his memoirs were promptly and politely declined. On the side of the Bank of England, the almost complete silence was, for one hundred years, deafening. Something had gone seriously wrong and no one was encouraged to enquire about it. Here lay a mystery, which, at last, has been laid to rest.

A Tale of the River Bank

In October 1908, Kenneth Grahame's masterpiece, *The Wind in the Willows*, was published by Methuen. It was broadly dismissed by the critics and indeed, if it had aimed to be, as it became, one of the pearls of English literature for children, it is a very odd story indeed. The story centres on the adventures of a reckless, arrogant and foolish country gentleman in the form of a repulsive amphibian, Mr Toad of Toad Hall and his three close animal friends, Mole, Rat and Badger. Mole opens the story, revelling in emerging from his underground chambers into the sunshine, and is clearly Kenneth Grahame himself, announcing his escape from servitude in Threadneedle Street.

The Water Rat, based on Kenneth's younger brother, Roland, is passionate about his river bank habitat and the joy of 'messing about in boats' and Badger, the 'big stick' enforcer of order in the Wild Wood nearby, seems to be based on Hammond 'Brock' Chubb, Secretary of the Bank for 30 years from 1864 to 1894 and the man who approved the recruitment of Kenneth Grahame in 1879, gave him 100% (unparalleled in the Bank before or since) in the Entry Examinations, and who sponsored his appointment as Deputy Secretary.

By 1908, the year of publication of *The Wind*, Chubb was long gone from the Bank but fondly remembered. Roland the Rat, known as Ratty, however was alive and well and pursuing his own successful career through the Bank. He entered Bank service on 14 December 1882, retired as the Principal of the Private Drawing Office on 17 November 1927 and died suddenly on 11 October 1929.

This leaves a question. If all four characters were based on real-life people working in the Bank of England, who then was the despicable Mr Toad of Toad Hall, the rich, idle country squire who let his friends down. A boasting, lying, thieving villain, he was sent to gaol for twenty years for theft, dangerous driving and impertinence with the rural police. He quickly escaped in the clothes of a washerwoman – a strangely lovable character for his all too human foibles – fantasising with over-the-top enthusiasms, known for chatting up women, young and old, feasting and entertaining lavishly, mounting expeditions, dressing up and travelling in disguise. He spends freely and takes undue risks – restoring a houseboat, investing heavily in single racing sculls, lavishly fitting out a horse-drawn caravan, jumping off the footplate of a steam locomotive and, worst of all, at the wheel of a large, fast, luxurious motorcar that he had just stolen. Could this, by any chance, have been a Governor of the Bank of England?

There is evidence that Grahame did not get on with William Campbell Middleton (Governor 1907–9) as well as he had with the five previous Governors. Middleton was intent on further rationalisation of the Bank and seemed to regard the well-entrenched Grahame as an obstacle in his path. Responsible for the staff, the fabric of the buildings, the organisation of the Court of Directors and the general administration of the Bank, Grahame had also carried through a thorough overhaul of staff salaries and conditions with new rules (1902-6) covering appointments, promotions and the classification of staff. He had also been responsible for the purchase and development of the site of the Bank of England Sports Club and the Bank of England Records Office at Roehampton, both of which opened in 1908. In his subsidiary role as Private Secretary to the Governor, he had been well rewarded with bonuses (the last in 1907) and testimonies of good service. In 1905 he had been given the Presidency of the immensely prestigious and time-consuming BELLA, the Bank of England Library and Literary Association, founded and richly endowed in

1850, a clear indicator that he was highly respected and earmarked for further tenure of high office.

There is, however, another much stronger candidate for the role of Mr Toad – a larger-than-life future Governor, then a curmudgeonly Director, waiting in the wings.

Walter Cunliffe

A piece of evidence, remaining in the Bank of England for 100 years, points straight to Walter Cunliffe who became a Director of the Bank in 1895, Deputy Governor in 1911 and Governor in 1913 to March 1918 when a fierce row with the Chancellor of the Exchequer forced his resignation. He was of an autocratic, aggressive, unpredictable and bullying nature, widely hated by senior management in the Bank. Outside, he was known as 'The Tyrant of the City' and was frequently lampooned by the press. Nonetheless, through World War I he provided strong leadership and won some important battles with the Government. In 1918 Cunliffe proved a disastrous choice as chairman of a commission on currency and foreign exchange which was examining the options to maintain the gold standard. On the question of setting the level of reparations to be imposed on Germany for damage during World War I, he spoke airily of $120 billion, while John Maynard Keynes, the Treasury spokesman at the Versailles Peace Conference, put the German capacity to pay at $10 billion. The official history of the Bank of England (Sayers) describes him waspishly as having 'the advantage of knowing his own mind, perhaps not a very difficult one to know'. His pleasures were traditional country pursuits: according to the Oxford Dictionary of National Biography, 'he hunted and fished, shot game large and small, and farmed as a gentleman should', qualities of little appeal to the like of Kenneth Grahame.*

* For more on Grahame consult www.kennethgrahamesociety.net

'You Are No Gentleman, Sir!'

The official reason given for Kenneth Grahame's departure from the Bank was ill-health. He produced a Harley Street consultant's report which diagnosed arteriosclerosis with symptoms of insomnia, constant headache, amnesia, depression and nervous breakdown. The Bank Medical Officer examined Grahame and simply reported that he could find no loss of memory or mental impairment. Both letters are held in the Bank of England archive and were shown to Peter Green whose outstanding, detailed biography of Grahame was published in 1959. Unmentioned in the biography and probably not shown to Green was a letter in the archive from Marston Acres, the distinguished archivist of the Bank and author of a two-volume book about the Bank published in 1931. He had worked closely with Grahame, particularly at the time of Grahame's abrupt departure. He writes:

> *All that I can be aware about is that his retirement had nothing to do with ill-health but to his resentment of the bullying nature of a Director with whom he was discussing some official business, when he was provoked into saying: 'You are no gentleman, sir!'.*
>
> *I believe the Director concerned in this episode was Walter Cunliffe (afterwards Lord Cunliffe) whose overbearing manner made him the terror of high officials in later years when he was Governor.*
>
> *The retirement was very sudden, as I believe Mr Grahame did not appear at the Bank again after the day the incident happened. Evidently his remark was immediately reported to the Governors, and he was probably told to absent himself from the Bank until the Court had considered the matter, when he was retired and granted the not very liberal pension of £400 per annum.**
>
> Signed W Marston Acres

* Also retained in the Bank archive is the Bank's calculation of Grahame's entitlement to an Early Retirement Pension on Account of Sickness. Under existing regulations, on his salary of £1,700 pa, he was due a pension of £791 pa. So Grahame only received one-half of his entitlement.

How 'The Wind' Came to be Written

In 1904 Kenneth Grahame began telling bedtime stories to his four-year old son, Alastair, whom he habitually addressed and referred to as 'Mouse'. Whenever he was away from home, which was often and sometimes for long periods, Grahame continued the stories by letter. The first letter about Rat, Mole and, incongruously, a Giraffe is dated May 1904. The first reference to Toad is in a story dated June 1904 entitled *The Tale of Mr Toad* ('a most unpleasant gentleman'). Alastair's governess, Miss Stott, made a habit of collecting the Toad letters and preserving them. It was she who first suggested to Kenneth that they would make a splendid children's book. Yet the book in its final form is such a hotch-potch of the original stories and later commentary that it is quite a hard book to read. Most children who like it – and very many do to this day – learn to skip over the incomprehensible bits, probably mystified by chapters such as *The Piper at the Gates of Dawn* (an encounter with the Nature God Pan) or *The Return of Ulysses.*

A Murderous Attack

As far as Grahame's brilliant career at the Bank was concerned, a significant turning point occurred on 24 November 1903, when a member of the public burst into Grahame's room and fired three shots at him. The man was over-powered by a quick-witted messenger using a fire hydrant and it transpired that all three shots had missed their target. Nonetheless, Grahame was very badly shaken by this experience. The assailant, a well-known anarchist called Robinson, was handed over to the police, declared to be a lunatic and committed to Broadmoor high-security prison on indefinite term.

Increasing Strain at Home and at Work

Meanwhile, Kenneth Grahame was facing an increasing workload and strain at work. His Deputy was frequently absent on sick-leave and the multiple duties of maintaining a large staff and resident families numbering at times close to 40 in total in buildings many of which were 150 years old were compounded by representational duties, welcoming royalty and visiting heads-of-state and a stream of other VIPs from the UK and abroad and being responsible for all luncheons, dinners and other events involving the Governors and Court of Directors.

Through these final five years at the Bank, in 1903 to 1908, Grahame suffered considerable ill-health including pneumonia and an operation. At home, his wife, ever a worrier, had health problems of her own. There were family disputes. As he put it in chapter 9 – *Wayfarers All*, 'the domestic storm-cone was hoisted' and Grahame began to fantasise, like the Sea-Going Rat ('I shipped myself on board a small trading vessel bound from Constantinople') of escape from the marital chains to freedom in the Mediterranean. Alastair, born in 1900 blind in one eye and with a stigma in the other, required attention. By 1907, the new Governor was growing impatient with Grahame's frequent bouts of illness, sick-leave, family problems and his shortened hours in the Bank (ten until four).

By late-1907, both Grahame and the Bank seemed to be gradually moving towards an acceptance that an early retirement might be a good idea. There were many precedents and the Bank had a long and enviable record of dealing generously with sickness and early pensions. But the bruising confrontation in June 1908 with Cunliffe and the humiliation of Grahame's departure changed everything.

Kenneth Grahame had certainly feared such an explosion. His *Bertie's Escapade* written in 1907 about the family pig and Alastair's two pet rabbits, has a theme of rejection and imminent redundancy, carrying the leitmotif 'Turn him out! Turn him out!' In *Bertie's Escapade*, Kenneth Grahame had found a formula to express his own anxieties and feelings as an overlay on a simple children's story. Here was the model for expressing his disappointment in real life through the rambling plot and somewhat implausible characters of *The Wind in the Willows*.

Reviewers and critics were slow to point out the broader contemporary political background reflected in *The Wind*. Edwardian fears of imminent conflict with Germany were compounded by a public paranoia about the presence of many German spies in London and, allegedly, throughout the country and empire; the arms race transformed by new technology such as the first *Dreadnought* battleship launched in 1906 and the perfecting of the Maxim heavy machine-gun, are mirrored in the subversive activities of the weasels and stoats and their successful invasion of Toad Hall.

Equally the environmental and countryside preservation movement picked up resonance from Grahame in his references to noisy and pollutant vehicles, the carving-up of the countryside by new surfaced roads and the influx of strangers brought by the new railways and steam passenger services on the river.

Riots on the streets, strikes in the dockyards, hunger marches and gatherings of agricultural labourers in the county towns were also of considerable concern to the public of the day and particularly to the Bank of England, well-fortified and armed with the Bank Picquet, a nightly squad of foot-soldiers and by day with its own militia of Volunteers, armed and trained in case of such eventualities.

The BELLA and The Old Lady

As expounded elsewhere in this volume, an important feature of understanding the Bank of England is not merely to listen to what it says, but to listen carefully to what it does not say.

Take for example the sumptuous literary quarterly *The Old Lady of Threadneedle Street* launched by the new Governor, Montagu Norman in March 1921. On the departure of Kenneth Grahame in 1908, Montagu Norman had taken over from him as President of the Library and Literary Association, BELLA, and greatly expanded its annual celebrity lecture-list, its special purchases of new books for the expanding library and refurbished the comfortable facilities of the new reading-room. Yet here lay a problem. The greatest literary figure ever to emerge from the Bank of England was one Kenneth Grahame, then enjoying considerable fame through what became a 24-year retirement from the Bank until his death in 1932. Sales of *The Wind in the Willows* in the UK were running at 80,000 per annum and indeed the book has never been out of print since then. Its popularity in the United States and through the English-speaking world was matched by many translations and editions printed overseas. Its rendering in 1929 by AA Milne into a play, *Toad of Toad Hall,* gave a tremendous new boost to sales establishing a tradition of regular professional Christmas productions each year in the West End, and its widespread performance by amateur dramatic companies all over the UK that persists to this day. A succession of feature films have fed this mainly juvenile appetite.

So how did the Bank of England celebrate this success by one of its most famous sons? One would expect *The Old Lady* to carry the sort of short literary pieces by Grahame that he was publishing elsewhere; interviews and reports on his public lectures might be expected; certainly photographs of him as he would be remembered vividly by the generation of Bank staff who had joined the Bank since 1890 and who were still working there in the 1920s and by many pensioners who had worked with him over the 30 years between his arrival in 1878 and departure in 1908.

I have examined carefully every one of the first 46 quarterly issues of *The Old Lady* and cannot find a single article, letter, review or photograph relating to Kenneth Grahame or *The Wind in the Willows*. In Issue 47 dated September 1932, he appears in the Obituary list as:

Kenneth Grahame (Formerly Secretary) Entered the Service, 12th December, 1878. Pensioned, 2nd July, 1908. Died, 6th July, 1932.

There is a most curious wording in the short announcement in the Editorial Notes of Issue No 47 which reads:

Mr Kenneth Grahame

Pensioners who live many years after their retirement from the Bank, and who seldom visit the scene of their former activities, are apt to be forgotten except by the few with whom they were intimate; but the passing of Mr Kenneth Grahame concerns not only those who knew him as a Bank Official, but all who have read and loved his books. We are glad to be able to include in this issue of The Old Lady a brief memoir of this distinguished author, and we have to thank Mrs Grahame for so kindly enabling us to reproduce a portrait of her husband.

The brief memoir is by his colleague, friend and consistent supporter, W Marston Acres, author of the letter quoted earlier. He begins:

'As more than 24 years have passed since Mr Grahame retired from the position of Secretary of the Bank of England, only the more senior members of the Staff will have memories of him as a bank official, but all who are lovers of literature will share in the general feeling of regret

that so brilliant a man has passed from the world, and will be proud to recognise that Mr Grahame has, by his writings, conferred a distinction on the institution of which he was a member comparable to that with which Charles Lamb honoured the East India House.'

Missing is any mention of his achievements during ten years of service in one of the top three jobs in the Bank. Marston Acres goes on to describe his own early experiences of working with and for Kenneth Grahame:

'It was my privilege, when a junior in the service of the Bank, to come into personal contact with Mr Grahame both before and after his appointment as Secretary, and I have pleasant recollections of many small kindnesses he shewed to me and of the considerate manner in which he criticised my early efforts to adapt the Queen's English to the purposes of official letters. My impression of Mr Grahame was of a shy, reserved man, with a fine presence and charm of manner, who did not fit in with my pre-conceived notions of a bank official; but I had no idea that he was then engaged in writing the books which would gain for him a world-wide reputation, although I listened carefully to some advice he once gave me on the subject of punctuation and the construction of sentences.'

Then Marston Acres, surprisingly, omits any reference to Kenneth Grahame's achievements within the Bank or of his own later involvement with Kenneth Grahame. There is almost a lacuna in the text. Perhaps these paragraphs were edited out of the published version.

He goes on:

'This is not the place, nor is mine the pen, to attempt an estimate of Mr Grahame's literary qualities, but there cannot be many people who need to be persuaded that The Golden Age, Dream Days *and* The Wind in the Willows *are books which have enriched our literature. It is given to but few 'grown-ups' to have so sympathetic an understanding of the child-mind and, at the same time, to be so splendidly equipped with the gift of humour and a facility for expression as to be*

able to communicate to others through the medium of the written word, as Mr Grahame was able to do, something of the delight which children experience in a world which seems to offer them limitless adventures.

'Amongst those who have served the Bank there have not been wanting men with definite literary gifts, and if Robert Browning's father[*] *had not been so indulgent a parent it is probable that the Bank might have been able to claim the great Victorian poet as an employee; but it was left for the 19th century to produce the man who was to be both an official of the Bank and a literary artist of the first rank, and the name of Kenneth Grahame will always be held in high honour by the 'Old Lady of Threadneedle Street' and those who serve her.'*

Appended are three short tributes from *The Times, The Church Times* and *The Week-end Review,* all focussing on the literary achievement of Kenneth Grahame and without any mention whatsoever of the Bank of England or Grahame's connection with the Bank.

Grahame's Part in the Official History of the Bank

In the three-volume official history of the Bank of England between 1891 and 1944 published by Cambridge University Press in 1976, there is a most detailed explanation and analysis of the staff remuneration, recruitment and advancement reforms instituted in 1902 to 1906. There is no mention of Kenneth Grahame, who, as Secretary, was responsible for them. Indeed the only reference to Grahame in the entire text reads as follows:

'Even in the more responsible posts a man of intellectual capacity often found his mind only half-employed: Kenneth Grahame, for example, was able to write The Wind in the Willows *and other books while he rose to be, and was for ten years, Secretary of the Bank. There were*

* who completed 50 years' service in the Bank of England as a gentleman-clerk. At the time and up to quite recently, it was quite normal for members of the Bank staff to nominate their sons for Bank service.

many others who were quietly exercising imagination and talents which were varied but found no expression in the art of central banking.'

A Bank Ghost Laid to Rest

Only as the centenary of *The Wind in the Willows* approached in 2008, was it decided appropriate to mount a small display-cabinet covering the book in the back of the Bank of England Museum. Also displayed were the conflicting medical reports on Grahame from the Harley Street consultant and the Bank doctor, the original calculation of what Grahame was entitled to under the Bank's Pension rules and, for the very first time, the letter of Marston Acres identifying Walter Cunliffe as the reason for his departure.

Most probably, either Cunliffe or Grahame or both simply lost their temper and, because of the public nature of the occasion, the Court of Directors was obliged, willy-nilly, to defend the senior man, the Director at the expense of the more junior employee.

High Stakes

Another question is whether the Bank was put under any pressure by this issue. Had they had serious misgivings about the themes of *Bertie's Escapade* and *The Wind in the Willows?* Was the Government or the Foreign Office involved?

It would be useful to know whether the Bank knew about *The Wind in the Willows* before Kenneth Grahame left it. I suspect they did, as the search for a publisher involved a wide range of people and was extended over several months. It must have been common tittle-tattle in the literary drawing-rooms of the West End and in the City banking parlours and watering holes that the distinguished Secretary of the Bank and well-known Author was trying, with difficulty, to launch a third masterpiece.

My researches over the last 20 years drew me to the difficulties Grahame faced in finding a publisher. They have thrown up some very strange facts and some very unlikely people. Let us restrict ourselves here to just three of them: Theodore Roosevelt, President of the United States, Kaiser Wilhelm of Germany and the highly successful author of the Christopher Robin stories, AA Milne.

Kaiser Wilhelm

Kaiser Wilhelm had been dazzled by *The Golden Age* and had quoted and praised it in public. On one occasion he announced that he had only two books in his cabin on his yacht *Hohenzollern* – the Bible and *The Golden Age*. Mercifully he did not go on to say which he preferred.

Given the public hysteria in 1900–14 concerning German spies in London, the arms race and the competition for new colonies in Africa, had it been known in what high esteem the Secretary of the Bank of England was held by the Kaiser, alarm bells would have been ringing all over the Bank, the City and Whitehall.

President Roosevelt

Theodore Roosevelt was deeply smitten by *The Golden Age* (1895) and *Dream Days* (1898), both immediate best-sellers in the UK and the USA. He wrote several times to Grahame to congratulate him and to beg Grahame to go and stay with the Roosevelt family in Washington in the White House. Did Grahame tell the Bank about these invitations from a most powerful head-of-state? Probably not, but if not, was he in breach of Bank security?

In late 1907 when the bulk of the text of *The Wind in the Willows* was complete, Kenneth Grahame still had the greatest difficulty in finding a publisher. With two best-sellers under his belt, this came as a great surprise. Bodley Head turned him down flat and his literary agent, Curtis Brown worked hard to find an alternative but without success, and wrote:

'I tried it with magazine editors all over England and America. They thought it too fantastic and wouldn't have it.'

Finally, Grahame sent a copy of the text to Roosevelt describing it in a letter:

'Its qualities, if any, are mostly negative – i.e. – no problems, no sex, no second meaning – it is only an expression of the very simplest joys of life as lived by the simplest beings of a class that you are specially familiar with and will not misunderstand.'

Roosevelt immediately wrote to a publisher friend, Charles Scribner, saying:

'...it is such a beautiful thing that you must publish it.'

As a result, Methuen reluctantly agreed to take it, but refused to pay a guaranteed advance, as was normal. In compensation and because they were convinced they were taking on a turkey, they offered 'excellent rising royalties, just in case the book should fulfil their dreams'. The immediate beneficiary of this error of judgement was, of course, Kenneth Grahame but today it is the Bodleian Library in the University of Oxford to whom Grahame's copyright eventually reverted.

AA Milne

Roosevelt entered the public domain regarding *The Wind,* when AA Milne produced a new Foreword and included in full a letter from Roosevelt to Grahame dated January 17

1909 describing how the two elder Roosevelt boys seized hold of the book and took great delight in it and how his wife read it aloud to the younger children:

'Now I have read it and re-read it, and have come to accept the characters as old friends...'

AA Milne then concludes his Introduction as follows:

'The book is a test of character. We can't criticize it, because it is criticizing us. As I wrote once: It is a Household Book; a book which everyone in the household loves, and quotes continually; a book which is read aloud to every new guest and is regarded as the touchstone of his worth. But I must give you one word of warning. When you sit down to it, don't be so ridiculous as to suppose that you are sitting in judgment on my taste, or on the art of Kenneth Grahame. You are merely sitting in judgment on yourself. You may be worthy: I don't know. But it is you who are on trial.'

A Lively Oral Tradition

This brings me to the point of the title of this chapter. *The Wind in the Willows* is about many things. It is most certainly about the Bank and it was the Bank of England that was on trial. Gagged by the Court of Directors and by convention, Grahame had found an appropriate medium for expressing his dismay and frustration. Any Bank of England man or woman reading or re-reading *The Wind in the Willows* will spot the jokes, the wit and the irony of Bank life. There was also a lively oral tradition in the Bank that Grahame picked up perfectly. Take the lively office parties round Christmas and the New Year where the cabaret would frequently feature incidents in the book, lampooning, with apparent impunity, the Principal, Deputy and the Superintendents.

Or take the use of nicknames. Fifty years or so ago, I was nicknamed shortly after my arrival (for no reason known to me) Squire and within my immediate acquaintance were Ratty, Lefty, Otter as in 'otter and 'otter, Mole, Weasel, Ant and Hoppy, although I never knew a Toad. The messengers had, between themselves, their own sets of nicknames, often, in British military tradition, based on places of origin. Down at the Sports Club, nicknames were used extensively to confuse the visiting team. In the downtrodden and seething typing-pools and filing and note-processing sections, women muttered darkly to each other in a coded language of their own.

Massive Quantitative Easing

So what has *The Wind in the Willows* to do with the future of the Bank of England? As you might have guessed from the foregoing, if you can believe me, quite a lot.

Mole, in the opening paragraph of the book resolves to give up all whitewashing, that ancient, highly-developed and highly-prized Bank of England craft, and decides spontaneously to abandon 'his dark and lowly little house with its spirit of divine discontent and longing'. Toad rounds off the story with a full rehabilitation of Toad Hall, massive quantitative easing in the form of a banquet for all (the best of everything') and a reluctant paying-off of outstanding debts and obligations.

The rabbits are unreliable and inefficient tax-collectors; the field-mice, young, nervous and fearful members of the public. The hedgehogs protect the Master when he is asleep in his office; the Badger 'gave them sixpence apiece and a pat on the head, and they went off with much respectful swinging of caps and touching of forelocks'.

The Benefits of Being Underground

Later, Mole and Badger are in total agreement on the benefits of living underground; 'Nothing can happen to you, and nothing can get at you. You're entirely your own master, and you don't have to consult anybody or mind what they say', says Mole to which Badger replies 'There's no security, or peace and tranquillity, except underground... No builders, no tradesmen, no remarks passed on you by fellows looking over your wall. And, above all, no weather'.

This is the mere first clue in an archaeological dig. Like the ruins of the ancient city which Mole had discovered buried beneath his bank, there is a whole treatise on the fundamentals of central banking to be excavated here.

The Ducks' Ditty on Bank Supervision

As the Bank of England will shortly resume responsibility for major aspects of Banking Supervision, it is relevant to note Grahame's commentary on certain financial operators whose 'ducking and diving' has recently become a matter of intense concern to the population in general, particularly the youngsters at the nesting stage of their lives:

All along the backwater,
Through the rushes tall,
Ducks are a-dabbling,
Up-tails all !

Ducks' tails, drakes' tails,
Yellow feet a-quiver,
Yellow bills all out of sight
Busy in the river !

Slushy green undergrowth
Where the roach swim –
Here we keep our larder,
Cool and full and dim.

Every one for what he likes!
We like to be
Heads down, tails up,
Dabbling free!

High in the blue above
Swifts whirl and call –
We are down a-dabbling,
Up tails all!

'I don't know that I think so very much about that little song, Rat,' observed the Mole cautiously. He was no poet himself and didn't care who knew it; and he had a candid nature.

'Nor don't the ducks neither,' replied the Rat cheerfully. 'They say, "Why can't fellows be allowed to do what they like when they like and as they like, instead of other fellows sitting on banks and watching them all the time and making poetry and things about them? What nonsense it all is!" That's what the ducks say.'

'A Real Gentleman'

In the two last paragraphs of *The Wind in the Willows,* Kenneth Grahame is determined to have the final word on the circumstances of his dismissal and on ensuring the future of the Bank of England. The altered but unrepentant Toad is said, with heavy irony, to be 'holding himself as an instrument of Fate, sent to punish fat women with mottled arms **who couldn't tell a real gentleman when they saw one**'.

'The Terrible Grey Badger'

Grahame then goes on to describe how the four friends, Badger, Mole, Ratty and Toad 'would in the course of long summer evenings, take a stroll together in the Wild Wood, now successfully tamed as far as they were concerned; and it was pleasing to see how respectfully they were greeted by the inhabitants'. The mother-weasels would bring their young to the mouths of their holes and 'when their infants were fractious and quite beyond control, they would quiet them by telling how, if they didn't hush them and not fret them, the terrible grey Badger would up and get them'.

'This was a base libel on Badger, who, though he cared little about Society, was rather fond of children; **but it never failed to have its full effect.**'

PART SEVEN

Coping with Crisis and Upheaval

From the Governor on the Outbreak of War in 1939

'a community effort for the public good'

If I may claim – as I do – to have been from the beginning some sort a Godfather to the *'Old Lady'*, it will be easy to understand why I am writing this note. The occasion demands it – the first issue in time of war. Of this unique event some notice should be taken, not least by our subscribers.

I realise that all large groups of people have been of late much scattered; and this is entirely true of our own community of Bank men and Bank women. The process is not yet complete and no useful consensus can yet be taken; but let us look at these rough figures: Nearly four hundred of us are serving, in one place or another, as sailors, soldiers or airmen; nearly a hundred and fifty – men and women – are working in the Midlands and half that number in the outer fringe of London; over a thousand are lodged in Hampshire (where the measure of comfort will, I hope, before long equal that of health) and over two thousand remain at the Branches and Offices in London.

Although divided for the time and confronted, many of us, with unfamiliar problems and conditions, let us retain, for all we may, the sense of a community of effort for the public good. In keeping us together and aware each of the other's circumstances, the *'Old Lady'* has a part to play. I hope that she will be just as determined as we all are to fly her standard high, and that her circulation will increase around the wider field.

Those of us who are still unmolested in this Island yield pride of place to those on service, here or in France, at sea or in the air. No one would expect war to bring ease or pleasure or riches; to most of us this war has already brought some dis-ease, for various reasons and in varying degrees. But we are all determined, each in his or her own way, to carry our head high and to play our part with even temper until the end.'

Montagu Norman
15 November 1939

Montagu Norman served as Governor from 1920 to 1944. In April 1921 he launched the new quarterly, The Old Lady of Threadneedle Street *which survived and prospered in more or less the same format and under the same mandate until December 2007.*

From the Governor after the End of the War in 1945

'a tradition of service that is wholly admirable'

'This is a fitting occasion for me to pay a tribute to that fine body of men and women (for there are more women than men) of the Bank of England who are doing a great job in a great way, combining together to make one of the most loyal and efficient organisations in the world. In speaking in their praise to-night I can do so without embarrassment, for I make no claim to have had much to do with the creation of the Organisation as it exists today. But I recognise loyalty when I see it, and I am no mean judge of efficiency. I am proud to be their Governor: for, my Lord Mayor, it is not the great building across the Street that is the Bank of England – it is the people within it, those who, in war and in peace, carry on its day-to-day work with a tradition of service that is wholly admirable and of whom too little is known: for it has been more exciting, although less accurate, to criticise the Bank rather than to praise it.'

Lord Catto,
Governor 1944 to 1949

From the Governor's remarks at a dinner given by the Lord Mayor of London to the Bankers and Merchants of the City on 3 October 1945, in which he outlined the formidable task of bringing home the departments evacuated to the country during the War and the challenge of absorbing the large number of staff returning from military service.

Mervyn King

Governor of The Bank of England
Address to the 2010 Trades Union Congress, Manchester
Wednesday 15 September 2010

President and Congress

Recent times have indeed been turbulent. After a decade and a half of stability, with rising employment and living standards, came the crisis and recession – the biggest economic upheaval since the Great Depression. Before the crisis, steady growth with low inflation and high employment was in our grasp. We let it slip – we, that is, in the financial sector and as policy-makers – not your members nor the many businesses and organisations around the country which employ them. And although the causes of the crisis may have been rooted in the financial sector, the consequences are affecting everyone, and will continue to do so for years to come.

Thankfully, the costs of the crisis have been smaller than those of the Great Depression. But only because we learnt from that experience. An unprecedented degree of policy stimulus, here and abroad, prevented another world slump. Even so, around a million more people in Britain are out of work than before the crisis. Many, especially the young unemployed, have had their futures blighted. So we cannot just carry on as we are. Unless we reform our economy – rebalance demand, restructure banking, and restore the sustainability of our public finances – we shall not only jeopardise recovery, but also fail the next generation.

To my mind, a market economy and its disciplines offer the best way of raising living standards. But a market economy cannot survive on incentives alone. It must align those incentives to the common good. It must command support among the vast majority who do not receive the large rewards that accrue to the successful and the lucky. And it must show a sense of fairness if its efficiency is to yield fruit.

There was nothing fair about the financial crisis. It was caused not by problems in the real economy; it came out of the financial sector. But it was the real economy that suffered and the banks that were bailed out. Your members, and indeed the businesses which employ them, are entitled to be angry. But however legitimate, anger will not produce change unless its energy is harnessed to a cool analysis of what happened and why. So I want to discuss the fundamental causes of the crisis before turning to current policy.

The fall of the Berlin Wall in 1989 changed both politics and economics. Within a few years, the former Soviet empire, China and other Asian economies, with their combined workforce of over a billion people, entered the world trading system as market economies. Their focus on export-led growth allowed consumers in the West to enjoy rising living standards as the prices of traded goods fell. But the trade surpluses in emerging economies implied an outflow of capital. Relatively poor countries were lending money to richer western ones – the reverse of the traditional model of development. In the process, countries like China built up huge holdings of foreign assets – running into trillions of dollars – matched by equally huge debts in the deficit countries. Such massive imbalances were never likely to be sustainable, and so it proved.

If the first fundamental cause of the crisis was the scale of imbalances in the world economy, the second was the inability of our banking system to absorb such large inflows of capital without taking excessive risk. In the five years leading up to the crisis, the balance sheets of the West's largest banks doubled – mainly because banks lent more to other firms within the financial sector than to the wider economy. And the proportion of capital held by banks shrank so that their leverage – the ratio of total liabilities to equity capital – rose to unprecedented levels. Immediately prior to the crisis, the leverage ratios of some UK banks approached 50. To say that was risky is an understatement: at such levels, a 2 percent fall in the value of a bank's assets is sufficient to wipe out its capital and render it insolvent.

Remuneration, especially the structure of financial sector bonuses, encouraged excessive risk-taking, and distorted the aspirations and career choices of too many talented young people. Investors, banks and regulators had been swept up by the apparent success of modern finance. When investors realised that many of the assets that banks held on their balance sheets were opaque and hard to value, there was immediate and justifiable concern about the solvency of many of those banks.

At the end of 2008, these two fundamental factors culminated in the worst financial crisis in history. In the six months after Lehman Brothers collapsed world trade fell by nearly 20 percent – a faster decline than in the Great Depression. Around the world, the same telling phrase was repeated: economic activity was 'falling off a cliff'. In its statement to the London G20 summit in April 2009, the international trade union movement argued that 'The first priority for G20 leaders must be to restore confidence by halting the freefall in world growth'. That has been achieved. World output grew by 4 percent over the past year. And in the United Kingdom, growth has been somewhat faster than anticipated a year ago. Nevertheless, total UK output remains around 10 percent below where it would have been had the crisis not occurred.

So how do we prevent this happening again? If we are to prevent another crisis, action is required on both of the fundamental causes. First, we need to resolve the problems caused by massive capital flows from poor to rich countries. Yet the imbalances are growing again. This problem can be tackled only by international cooperation – most obviously through the G20 – and I hope that the trade union movement will continue to engage with that process.

Second, our financial system needs radical reform. Slowly but surely, we must move towards a banking system that does not put both the economy and your members' livelihoods at risk. In the long run, banks will have to hold much more capital and be much less highly leveraged. Part of the answer is improving the way we regulate banks, and devising policy tools to control the risks taken by the financial system as a whole. The aim should not be to prevent all bank failures. Just as with every other company in the economy, banks that get it wrong must be allowed to fail, without risk to ordinary depositors or taxpayers. In 2008, banks were bailed out not to protect them but to protect the rest of the economy from the banks. That may not seem fair – and it isn't – when other companies, such as Jaguar, had to stand on their own feet or go to the wall. So banks too must face market discipline.

But we need to do more than reform our banking system. If the world economy needs rebalancing, so does our own. The substantial trade deficit over a number of years means that national spending exceeded production. We need a higher national saving rate, a shift in spending and production away from consumption and towards exports. And a key part of that is a reduction in our budget deficit.

There is a perfectly reasonable debate about the precise speed at which to reduce the deficit. Indeed, I supported the extra fiscal stimulus to the economy provided in the immediate wake of the crisis. And there is a further question about how the deficit should be reduced – the balance between raising taxes and cutting spending. That is not for me to say; that is for you and the politicians to debate. But it is indisputable that, because of the crisis, national income is 10 percent lower than was expected with a damaging impact on tax revenues. As a result, this country has the largest peacetime budget deficit in its history – over 11 percent of GDP in the fiscal year to 2010. Although a large budget deficit is inevitable for a period after a crisis, it is also clearly unsustainable – our national debt, even relative to GDP, is rising sharply and will continue to do so for several years. It is vital for any government to set out and commit to a clear and credible plan for reducing the deficit. I would be shirking my responsibilities if I did not explain to you the risks of failing to do so.

Vague promises would not have been enough. Market reaction to rising sovereign debt can turn quickly from benign to malign, as we saw in the euro area earlier this year. It is not sensible to risk a damaging rise in long-term interest rates that would make investment and the cost of mortgages more expensive. The current plan is to reduce the deficit steadily over five years – a more gradual fiscal tightening than in some other countries. As a result of a failure to put such a plan in place sooner, some euro-area countries have found – to their cost – a much more rapid adjustment being forced upon them.

Of course, no one can forecast the gusts – or indeed storms – the economy may face looking ahead. But if the recovery is slower than expected then the automatic fiscal stabilisers – the lower tax receipts and higher spending that result from weaker growth – will act to stimulate demand. And monetary policy can react too, especially when there is a credible plan to reduce the deficit.

In the wake of the worst financial crisis ever, the amount of money in our economy – broad money – is now barely growing at all. It was the failure in the 1930s to halt a marked contraction in the money supply that led to the Great Depression. So the Bank of England has taken extraordinary measures – described as 'quantitative easing' – to boost the supply of money in order to support a recovery in the economy and keep inflation on track to meet our target. And because monetary policy is a flexible instrument that can be changed in either direction each month, it is the best tool for managing the economy in the short run.

Nevertheless, the road ahead is unlikely to be straight. There is considerable uncertainty about the prospects for both the United States and the euro area – our most important export markets. Business and consumer confidence at home has weakened recently, and it will be some time before our banking sector is able to finance a recovery on the usual terms. The transition to a better balanced economy will be difficult. But we are already seeing encouraging signs of expansion in manufacturing and UK exports.

This morning's figures show a small rise in the claimant count and a small fall in the Labour Force Survey measures of unemployment. But the big picture is that unemployment is higher than before the crisis but lower than many had feared a year ago. In July, on one of my regular visits to different parts of the country, I met with the Scottish TUC in Glasgow to learn more about the labour market there. Our contacts with experienced union officials in touch with a range of companies and sectors are the best source of intelligence on labour markets. With your help, we are determined to understand what is happening in every region and country of our economy so that we can set the right monetary policy. I want to assure you that the Bank of England is there to serve the whole economy, right across the length and breadth of this country.

The costs of this crisis will be with us for a generation. And we owe it to the next generation to seize this opportunity to put in place the reforms that will make another crisis much less likely and much less damaging. We at the Bank of England and you in the trade union movement should work together. It will require patience and determination on all our parts, including your members. But the prize of restoring and maintaining economic stability – and a return to sustained rises in employment and living standards – will be worth the effort.

Squash – The Central Banker's Game

Gordon Richardson
Governor of the Bank of England 1973–83

Squash should surely be the Central Banker's game *par excellence.* It appeals to his instincts in more than one respect. First, it is economical in resources – employing only two people, who play very hard for a short period, expend only human – and not significantly OPEC – energy and who then pass the court on to other players. I have reluctantly to accept a certain contrast in this respect to cricket which occupies great tracts of land and in which 22 people are nominally employed, but where restrictive practices prevent more than two from working together – or against each other – for most of the time, while the others stand or sit around idly. Second, the game should attract the Central Banker's admiration because Squash, like the City of London, depends largely on self-regulation. Just as in this country we have no bank inspectors and no SE, so Squash players generally sort out their differences without need for the referee's whistle or the umpire's white coat – although this is not to say that animated disputes never occur either on \ court or in the City. Perhaps the City should evolve some way of diffusing disputes analogous to asking for a 'let'. There is, I am bound to say finally, one point on which a Central Banker might have some reservation. Whereas Fives was invented as boys hit balls at some buttresses of Eton College Chapel, it is said that Squash was developed among the debtors locked up in the Fleet Prison. But the game has long thrown off any implication of 'rackets' (in the Chicago sense).

From The Old Lady at Play, *quoting a speech made on 13 July 1980.*

PART EIGHT

The Independence of the Bank of England

The impact of nationalisation on the Bank of England in 1946 was minimal. Successive British governments recognised the importance of the Bank of England as a substantial revenue earner for the British Government and were hesitant to interfere with this invaluable 'golden goose' or to compromise the accompanying rapid growth of the UK financial sector. The need for a firm Bank of England hand in managing the sterling exchange rate and the weakened UK balance of payments was never seriously questioned. Monetary policy and the control of inflation was a different matter with successive governments sometimes unsure of the fiscal and political implications of whatever Bank Rate was being decided by the Chancellor of the Exchequer in Great George Street and the Governor in Threadneedle Street.

The seminal re-thinking on the advisability of letting the Bank of England determine monetary policy independently by a combination of setting interest rates and intervention in the money markets came from Nigel Lawson in a memo to the Prime Minister, Margaret Thatcher, dated 25 November 1988. Then Chancellor of the Exchequer, he made it quite clear that it was for the Government to set a target inflation rate and it was for an independent committee of the Bank of England to deliver the appropriate monetary policy. With his permission, we reproduce below the text of his remarks followed by the relevant paragraphs in his updating chapter entitled Retrospect from 2010 included in his new *Memoirs of a Tory Radical* published in October 2010.

Mrs Thatcher was reluctant to implement the Lawson proposals, but on assuming office in 1997, the new Prime Minister, Tony Blair, went ahead with the creation of an independent Monetary Policy Committee within the Bank of England. In his autobiography, *A Journey*, published in September 2010, Tony Blair pays a generous tribute to the original Nigel Lawson proposals.

European Monetary Union and the Independence of the Bank of England

extracts from Memoirs of a Tory Radical *by Nigel Lawson, published 18 October 2010 by Biteback Press*

European Monetary Union

I had always been wholly opposed to European Monetary Union, not merely so far as UK participation is concerned, but indeed for Europe as a whole. In particular, the major speech I made as Chancellor in January 1989 sets out the case against it (the first time this had been done by any Minister), and I continued to do so after I had left office – most fully at an EMU conference in London in July 1995.

In the first place, it is always a mistake to undertake a major economic initiative for political rather than economic reasons. It is no secret that European Monetary Union is a political and not an economic project: designed to achieve a further major step on the road to a fully integrated Europe.

In an age of globalisation, the economic context is in any event global rather than regional, while in purely economic terms there can be little dispute that the imposition of a single monetary policy over an area as large and diverse as the European Union, with its many different languages, cultures and traditions, is undesirable.

I have consistently argued that monetary union, if it is to work at all satisfactorily, requires a high degree of fiscal union; and that, in a democracy, fiscal union inevitably demands a much greater degree of political union than the peoples of Europe – let alone the people of the UK – desire, or is indeed desirable. It is no historical accident that the evolution of the nation state and the evolution of the market economy coincided. For the market economy rests on a non-economic infrastructure, of which a vital component is the rule of law. And in a free society, the rule of law will work satisfactorily only if the people feel that, in the last resort, it is their law.

European Monetary Union nonetheless duly came into being when participating currencies – sterling, happily, not among them – were locked together at fixed rates on 1 January 1999. The formal birth of the Euro came exactly three years later. The unresolved but far from unpredictable Eurozone crisis of 2010 has, I fear, underlined the misgivings I have repeatedly expressed.

Bitter Conservative divisions over Europe, coupled with the party's inability to come to terms with the brutal (if necessary) rejection of Margaret Thatcher, and sterling's inglorious departure from the ERM (Exchange Rate Mechanism), (which lost the party its reputation for the competent conduct of economic policy), greatly helped Blair in his campaign to overcome the electorate's resistance to Labour. All this led to a Labour landslide victory in 1997 and, considerably assisted by Conservative incompetence in opposition, secured them a full 13 years of government.

New Labour and the Independence of the Bank of England

To a considerable extent, except towards the end, they *did* govern as new Labour, and conducted economic policy very much along the lines set out in this book. Its best and most important decision was taken right at the start: to confer independence on the Bank of England for the conduct of monetary policy, very much along the lines that I had unsuccessfully proposed to Margaret some nine years ealier. The Bank was given the single objective of meeting an inflation target, initially set at 2.5 percent, then from 2003 – when the Retail Price Index (RPI) was replaced by the Consumer Price index (CPI) – at 2 percent. While the immediate purpose may have been chiefly to disabuse any fears that the financial markets may have otherwise had that the incoming Labour government might – like its 1970s predecessor – be soft on inflation, the decision was a momentous one. It in effect institutionalised the proposition, which we had had such difficulty in sustaining in 1979, that the control of inflation was exclusively a matter for monetary policy, and not for either incomes policy or anything else, since monetary policy was the Bank's sole instrument.

The Conservative opposition's initial hostility to this move, a move which I publicly welcomed (Gordon Brown, the new Chancellor, asked me to do so : but I would have done so in any event), was exceedingly foolish, and fortunately soon abandoned. The Bank's remit was considerably easier than it would have been when I had advocated the move in 1988, since by 1997 inflation was already down to 2 per cent, with the result that its task was not that of getting inflation and inflationary expectations down, but the much less difficult one of keeping them down.

There was, of course, the practical question of what its guiding star should be. In chapter 23 I listed the four candidates: a nominal Gross Domestic Product (GDP) objective, a money supply target, a price level objective, and an exchange rate objective; and I described the practical problems with the first two of these. As between the second two, I had chosen the exchange rate, commenting that 'price-level rule works best when there is some authority removed from day-to-day political pressure, such as an independent central bank, which is free to choose its own method, but which is held strictly to account for the results achieved in terms of price stability.'

The newly independent Bank duly opted for this latter course of direct inflation targeting. Quite rightly in the circumstances. As the present Governor of the Bank of England, Mervyn King, has explained on a number of occasions, an important aspect of the conduct of monetary policy is influencing inflationary expectations, which requires market credibility. When inflation was as high as it was when we took office in 1979, with inflationary expectations rampant, and indeed for some time thereafter, a 2 percent inflation target would have had little if any market credibility, which is where the exchange rate came in. By 1997, with inflation already within the target range, it clearly did. And the Bank has carried out its task with considerable skill, establishing a valuable track record.

This extract is taken from Memoirs of a Tory Radical *by Nigel Lawson and is reproduced here with his permission. The final chapter, Retrospect from 2010, has sections on Politics 1989-1997; New Labour; The Economic Crisis 2008-10; Global Warming and Conclusions covering three fundamental principles for economic success, the absurdities of modern finance theory; the important political dimension; the task facing the new Coalition Government; and what democracy is essentially about.*

An Independent Central Bank

Minute by the Chancellor of the Exchequer, Rt Hon Nigel Lawson to the Prime Minister, Mrs Margaret Thatcher dated 25 November 1988

One of the most important achievements of this Government has been to place the defeat of inflation at the very heart of our economic policy. Although we are still only part of the way there, we have unequivocally reversed the rake's progress of the seventies and brought about a major cultural change.

I have been giving a great deal of thought to how we can best entrench that hard-won change, and make it a permanent feature of UK economic policy, while at the same time assisting us in the completion of our present task. I have reached the view that the best way to do this would be to give statutory independence to the Bank of England, charging it with the statutory duty to preserve the value of the currency, along the lines already in place and of proven effectiveness for the US Federal Reserve, the National Bank of Switzerland, and the Bundesbank.

Such a move would enhance the market credibility of our anti-inflationary stance, both nationally and internationally. It would make it absolutely clear that the fight against inflation remains our top priority; it would do something to de-politicise interest rate changes – though that can never be completely achieved; above all there would be the longer-term advantage that we would be seen to be locking a permanent anti-inflationary force into the system, as a counterweight to the strong inflationary pressures which are always lurking.

It would also, incidentally, make clear that we see a very different role for the Bank of England than absorption into some European central banking federation.

Clearly, since we have no written constitution, it would in theory be open for any future Government to repeal the legislation. But in practice there would be a powerful market sanction against that: the mere announcement of the intention to do so would in itself be so damaging to market confidence that any Government would be extremely reluctant to attempt it. And of course the longer the independent central bank had been in place, the more effective that sanction would be.

I have had some work done on this proposal by a very small, high-level group in the Treasury (I have not mentioned any of this to the Bank of England at this stage). It is clear that the move would be perfectly feasible. The heart of the scheme would consist of the following division of responsibilities:

1. The Bank would assume sole responsibility for the operation of monetary policy, with a statutory duty to protect and maintain the value of the currency. It would thus be responsible for setting short term interest rates and monetary targets
2. The Government would remain responsible for determining the exchange rate framework – for example, whether we were part of any international agreement, of whatever kind, formal or informal. The Bank would then be responsible for the conduct of exchange rate policy within that framework.

I have set out in an annexe a number of other points which would probably be necessary to define the new arrangement and ensure it worked successfully.

While there was of course a time, in the era of the gold standard, when the Bank of England possessed more independence than it enjoys today, there is no doubt that what I am proposing would constitute a radical change. But I believe it has substantial merit: it would provide a beneficial jolt to inflationary expectations and would help to lock into the body politic of this country a permanent anti-inflationary force. If you are content, the next step would be to bring the Bank of England into this discussion. My plan would be to publish a White Paper on Budget Day with the necessary legislation introduced in November 1989.

I should be happy to discuss this when we next meet.

Annexe – Further characteristics of an independent Bank of England

(i) The Bank would be obliged, as is the Bundesbank, to conduct monetary policy within the framework of the Government's economic policy as a whole, but only so far as that is consistent with its primary function of safeguarding the currency. There would also, and within this context, be a joint obligation on the Government and the Bank to work closely together in the conduct of economic policy.

(ii) The Treasury would be responsible for funding the Government's borrowing requirement(or for buying in debt when the Government was in surplus). But it would not be permitted to do this in a way which added to money or liquidity – *i.e.* it would have to sell longer-term instruments.This is the arrangement followed in Germany.

(iii) A portion of the reserves would be available to the Bank for use in intervention, but the Government would be able to set limits on total intervention (in either direction) and the Bank would have to obtain the Government's agreement before those limits were exceeded.

(iv) The Bank would, at least for the being, retain responsibility for supervising the banking system and the wholesale and gilt-edged markets. It would, of course, continue to discharge traditional central banking functions such as issuing notes and acting as the banker's bank.

(v) We should probably need to make the Bank of England answerable to Parliament in the sense that the Governor would appear regularly before a suitable Select Committee. But we would want this to be set up in a way which did not subject the Bank to unwarranted Parliamentary pressure.

(vi) The Court would be made up, as now, of a Governor, Deputy Governor, Executive Directors and non-Executive Directors. They would be appointed by the Government, though there might well be a case for making the appointments of all but the Governor himself subject to the approval of the Select Committee. Members of the Court would be appointed for a long period, to ensure their independence – probably for a term of 8 years. The appointment could be arranged so that one new non-Executive member came up for appointment each year.

(vii) We should also take the opportunity of a new Bank of England Act to put the Bank's finances on a proper statutory footing.

Reproduced with the permission of Lord Lawson of Blaby PC

The Blair–Brown Proposals on The Bank of England

Announced on 6 May 1997

Tony Blair

(Prime Minister 1997–2007)

'Some months before the election, Gordon and I formed the desire to give monetary policy – *i.e.* setting of interest rates – over to the Bank of England. The so-called "independence" of the Bank had been a keen academic, economic and political debate going back decades. [...]

'In truth, too, as with the Bank of England independence, the broad framework on the economy, never mind anything else, was set by me.'

These extracts are taken from A Journey *by Tony Blair (Chapter 4 – Honeymoon) published in 2010 by Hutchinson.*

Gordon Brown

(Chancellor of the Exchequer 1997–2007 & Prime Minister 2007–10)

'For two years Ed Balls and I had planned independence, and in the week before the election, unknown to anyone, we had submitted a large dossier to the Treasury. We were therefore in a position to announce the entire policy within a few days of taking power. The original plan, written by Ed, remained intact.'

This extract is taken from Beyond The Crash – Overcoming The First Crisis of Globalisation *by Gordon Brown (Chapter 2 – The Crisis Foreseen: Lessons from the Asian Crisis) published in 2010 by Simon & Schuster UK Ltd.*

PART NINE

The Wit of the Old Lady 1932–2007

The Old Lady of Threadneedle Street was launched as a quarterly literary magazine and journal of record in March 1921 and survived in more or less the same format and under the same mandate until December 2007. It was the inspiration of the new Governor, Montagu Norman who had been President of the prestigious Bank of England Library and Literary Association (the BELLA*), a task he took over from Kenneth Grahame in 1908. In the decade after World War One, Montagu Norman devoted considerable effort to extending the scope of the annual programme of celebrity lectures, re-equipping the reading-room and ensuring a generous supply of new books, publications and purchases and bequests of high-value texts such as the Kelmscott Chaucer. A part of this plan was a new high-quality quarterly which gave many Bank staff opportunities to publish their creative material and provided ample space for reporting on all the many Bank sporting activities, societies – thirty or forty in number such as the BEODS (Operatic and Dramatic). Retirement tributes and obituaries were taken very seriously and give a multiple snapshot of the wide interests, travels, adventures and researches of members of the staff, as well as much detail about working conditions, secondments and career paths in and out of the Bank.

The Old Lady was not without unofficial rivals in the Bank. In 1924 *Horizon*, described in Bank documents as 'outrageous' was terminated after four issues by co-opting two of its founders onto *The Old Lady* publications committee. In 1930–1 *Outburst* survived ten manuscript, two cyclostyled and two printed issues before it was declared subversive and before the abrupt departure of the Editor. It was then decided that from 1932 each issue of *The Old Lady* would carry a 2-6 page section entitled *Flyleaf* as an anonymous outlet for wit, humour and protest. This released a deluge of light and scurrilous verse and many anecdotes and Bank-based fantasies. Since 1932, *Flyleaf* has appeared in every issue until the last in December 2007. Over time, the arrangement of *Flyleaf* featured long-standing and much-loved sections. Examples collected from *Shorts from Reports, By Shannon's Waters, A Last Look Round, Epitaphs, Overheard* and *Some Shorter Reports* are given below with finally *Dear Frost, the Last Letter to a Pensioner* dated December 2007, a series published (anonymously) by Tim Kidd in almost every one of the 87 issues since June 1986.

Another feature of *Flyleaf* and other parts of *The Old Lady* has been a succession of able cartoonists. Here we provide a selection by the late Basil Hone; a further 25 Basil Hone cartoons appear in *A Thread of Gold, Volume One of The Bank of England Bedside Book* published in 2008. No.1 among the illustrators of *The Old Lady* and *Threadneedle* is Danny Denahy, whose work is featured on the cover and illustrating the contents of both volumes of *The Bank of England Bedside Book,* the first three issues of *Threadneedle* and the four booklets of memoirs published previously by the Threadneedle Club.

'Government Spending, Bankers in Trouble, Crooks or Spies – or is it just the Fire Brigade?'

Celebrity Lectures in the Twenties

Through the 1920s, a programme of three or four celebrity lectures was arranged each winter by the Bank of England Library and Literary Association (the 'BELLA')*. They were advertised to members well in advance, were nearly always packed and were reported faithfully in *The Old Lady*. The speakers were well-known public figures. Topics ranged widely, for example:

1921 Professor Edward Cannan
The Rate of Interest

1922 Mr Seton Gordon
*The Cairngorm Mountains and their Birds***

1923 Mr Mallory
Mount Everest

1924 Mr J Dover Wilson
The Merchant of Venice

1925 Mr Seton Gordon FZS
*The Spitzbergen Archipelago***

1926 Alfred Noyes
The Spirit of Poetry

1927 Mr St John Ervine
The Press Gang and the Government

1928 Sir Arthur Salter
The League of Nations on Trial

1929 GK Chesterton
Dickens and Hard Times

Ian Hay
The English Sense of Humour

In addition, the Governor, Montagu Norman, used the occasion of the Annual General Meeting of the BELLA to deliver each year a serious analysis of the issues of the day, usually under the title 'The European Situation'.

Another regular divertissement was the tradition of retirement addresses by former members of the staff, which were delivered in St Margaret's, Lothbury to all friends and colleagues who cared to attend. In each case, the lecturer was presented with an elaborate, if not 'magnificent' testimonial signed by his closest colleagues and friends. Many of these impressions and anecdotes eventually reached the pages of *The Old Lady*.

*The BELLA, the Bank of England Library and Literary Association, was founded in 1850. The Court of Directors gave an initial £500 and regular annual grants thereafter for the purchase of books and converted the old Securities Office into sumptuous quarters. By January 1851, membership had grown to 600 and the number of volumes available for borrowing to 3,500. By 1921, membership was barely more at 638, but the number of volumes had swelled to 17,000 and the number of leading periodicals available in the Reading Room was over 40. The annual staff subscription to the BELLA remained at the same level of 10 shillings for over a century. In addition to the Lending Library, there was a Reference Library which was linked to other major libraries in London.

** with lantern slides.

'They say they're thinking of changing the name.'

Shorts from Reports

- A jolly soul – Heaven help us!
- A patient sufferer from pernicious inertia
- In his right sphere, he would be excellent
- Works so much in the dark, he would not notice an electricity cut
- Can make up anything except her mind
- Inquisitive – but not about the work
- Always right but rarely relevant
- A keen eye for inessential detail
- Her help in balancing the accounts always makes a difference
- He boasts that work comes naturally to him – never guilty of looking for it
- Adept at making sows' ears out of silk purses
- Cannot talk and work at the same time; he talks a lot
- Thinks there is no one like her – fortunately her assumption is correct
- Sees a joke once it has been explained

Extracts from Flyleaf *published quarterly in* The Old Lady *from 1932 to 2007.*

Some Shorter Reports

- In his right sphere, OK
- Display purposes only
- A man of few words
- Goes without saying
- She stoops to concur
- Slow but unsure
- Consistently trying
- Wants understanding
- Wet with bright intervals

Extracts from Flyleaf *published quarterly in* The Old Lady *from 1932 to 2007.*

A Last Look Round – Some Bank Fundamentals

Extracts from the last entry in the Flyleaf *pages in* The Old Lady.

The Future

- The less future we have, the more we worry about it
- There will be no pillars of salt in Threadneedle Street
- It may, possibly, all come out all right in the end, but it will certainly come out different
- It will pass – if only you will let it
- The lender gets the interest, but the borrower gets the fun
- When searching the sky for good omens, take care you don't fall in the ditch

People

- A man chases a woman until she catches him
- People will do anything for money – even honest work
- Unhappily, by the time one is old enough to have learnt restraint, there is nothing left to restrain
- When there is a struggle between the intelligence and the heart, the intelligent usually trust the heart

The Economy

- It's not a question of whether you are right, it's a question of whether you're covered
- Somehow or other one never asks a shopkeeper 'How little is that?'
- What you do in this world is of no consequence. The question is what you can make other people believe that you have done
- You can't make footprints in the sands of time by sitting down

Personal

- In the long run it pays best not to attempt to earn the good opinion of a bad man

Overheard

Over the 87 years of The Old Lady *– 347 quarterly issues published and one banned and withdrawn before it was published – there are many entries under the heading* Overheard. *Here are a few examples with a particular period flavour from the '20s, '30s, '40s, and '50s.*

Luncheon in the Bank Club

- 'Will my fried egg be long, Miss?' 'No, sir, round' (1928)
- 'Is this the green-pea or the ox-tail soup? It tastes like boiled soap' 'Oh that'll be the green pea; the ox-tail tastes like glue' (1929)

At the Annual Bank of England Art Show

- You often hear the expression: ' I can do that with my eyes shut' – now I am convinced that quite a number of people actually do (1938)

In the Air-Raid Shelter

- To find your girl in the dark, always feed her a pickled onion (1942)
- 'You told them I was a perfect fool?' 'Sorry about that, none of us is perfect' (1945)

In the Machine Room

- 'The trouble with mechanisation is finding enough people to operate the machines' (1948)
- 'Banking isn't my meteor' (1959)

'He had this wonderful idea of going out for a drink.'

Epitaphs

The art of the Epitaph, as befits The Old Lady, *flourished throughout the 87-year history of the quarterly Bank of England magazine extending from 4-liners in* Flyleaf *to entries of several pages containing hundreds of lines. Here is a small selection of the accompanying shorter epitaphs by Richard Powers and Frank Dancaster, both distinguished Editors of* The Old Lady.

For a Stickler Principal by Richard Powers

A man within this tomb resides
Of rectitude extensive
He worshipped virtue and besides
Vice is so expensive

For a Voluble Poetaster by Richard Powers

Here lies a man who went from bad to worse
From writing prose he turned to verse
Then, not content with Life, which let him write it
He tempted Fate and started to recite it

For An Unsuccessful Author by Frank Dancaster

For years he sent his MSS around
(The kind that every Editor forgets)
Now he contributes only to the ground
A circumstance no Editor regrets

For a Writer of Epitaphs by Frank Dancaster

He from the cankered body of the time
Cut, like a surgeon, folly, vice and crime
For he, diseased himself, with cunning art
Knew where to seek the most infected part

By Shannon's Waters

In each quarterly issue of The Old Lady *published between 1932 and 2007, the humour of the* Flyleaf *pages was enhanced by regular items which persisted for a decade or two. One of these through the 1950s was a flood of Bank-conceived and Bank-related limericks, based on Bank-related stories, gossip and easily recognised Bank characters. They always appeared under the title* By Shannon's Waters *and their authors were strictly anonymous. Here is a small selection.*

A militant spinster of Datchet
Never saw a silk hat but she'd snatch it
She would jump up and down
Till she ruined the crown
Then she'd slice up the brim with a hatchet

A young lady of Kensington Gore
Was, though pretty, a damnable bore
She would either confess
'Why, I couldn't care less!'
Or protest 'I could not agree more'

A scholarly schoolmarm of Hale,
Once counted the commas in Beyle
Although she scorned men-friends
She sometimes made pen-friends
With priggish Professors of Yale

An erudite grocer of Stroud
Read classical extracts aloud
Of a dubious kind
In the parlour behind
To a very peculiar crowd

'They say you'll feel better next year...'

Last Letter to a Pensioner
Tim Kidd, December 2007

Dear Frost,

Your kind offer of support, should I ever wish to apply to be Managing Director of the IMF, is much appreciated. However, with the entire staff of the Flyleaf Division busily packing their Bank-issue black dustbin liners, I feel it behoves me to appear to be equally distraught... Rather than jump ship to a lucrative job elsewhere, I have decided to build on my O level economics by doing a bit of work on my oft-postponed Nobel prize project. You will recall that I'm working on a back-of-the-envelope equation, a bit like $e=mc^2$, that will predict the velocity of circulation and output gap for the next thousand years. On Tuesday I thought I might tackle why underperforming economies underperform. That should leave me the rest of the week free to watch the cricket. A bit like our early days in the Registrar's Department, Frostie.

Yours terminally, George

Tim Kidd regularly wrote letters to Frost *and* Flyleaf *from June 1986 to December 2007.*

'Another Bank invitation – would I consider a five-year contract in Baghdad?'

PART TEN

Threadneedle Looks Back

Given the wealth of personal memoirs and other historical material in *The Old Lady of Threadneedle Street*'s 20,800 pages published between March 1921 and end-2007, we thought that the successor magazine and current series of bedside books should continue to act as a stimulus to Bank of England memoir writers and as a conduit for the product of their labours to be lodged ultimately in the Bank of England Archives so that the best of them are carefully preserved within the Bank. Our appeals to subscribers to *Threadneedle* and reminders to all Bank of England pensioners produced a healthy stream of material, some fine examples of which are reproduced here.

To keep the flow at a healthy level, we are going to need, as in the past, both reminders and incentives. Literary prizes have been offered by the Bank at intervals since the foundation of the BELLA in 1850 and continuously each year since 1950.

As part of the centenary celebrations of the BELLA in 1950, it was resolved to appoint each year a well-known literary figure to review all four quarterly issues of the previous year and to select a prize-winner. The prize, a quite modest sum, was presented to the winner by the judge for the year at a dinner held in the Bank of

England and his or her report was published in due course in *The Old Lady*. This system lasted for 41 years. The full list of winners and judges was included in *A Thread of Gold*, Volume One of this series. The judges included Sir Osbert Sitwell, Compton Mackenzie, John Betjeman, Sir Harold Nicholson, Lord David Cecil, Andre Maurois, JB Priestley, LP Hartley, Stephen Spender, John Lehmann, John Freeman, Victor Gollancz, Cecil Harmsworth King, Pamela Hansford Johnson, HE Bates, Bernard Levin, John Fowles, John Arlott, Antonia Fraser, Claire Tomalin, Laurie Lee, Peter Ustinov, William Rees-Mogg, Marghanita Laski, Paul Theroux, Katherine Whitehorn, Brian Johnston, Peter Porter, John Mortimer, Robert Robinson, Ned Sherrin and Joan Bakewell.

By September 1983, the Governors had put a new system in place to award annual prizes, incentives and sponsorships to *Old Lady* contributors out of a fund they had set up to commemorate the Editor, David Nye who, with his wife and three young daughters, perished in July 1983 in a helicopter accident in the Scilly Isles. The balance of that fund was handed to the Threadneedle Club in 2008 to help establish the successor magazine, *Threadneedle* and to help expand the membership of the Club.

We have in mind to reinstitute the earlier system with the selected literary judge and winner attending the annual Threadneedle Club Dinner or other Threadneedle event for the presentation of the prizes.

Meanwhile for the issues of 2008, 2009 and 2010 we have instituted a prize of £100 per annum each out of the funds we inherited from the David and Susan Nye Memorial Fund. The Chairman and Secretary were excluded from both the nominations and the voting while the five members of the judging panel, Peter J Bull, Peter Edgley, Rodney Galpin, Malcolm Gill and Jacquie Pearce were permitted to vote for each other, but not for themselves. The winners were:

2008 – Peter Edgley and Alan Watson (joint winners)
2009 – Roger Barnes
2010 – John Lowen

All four of the winning contributions are included in the first section below.

Winners of The Threadneedle Prize 2008–10

The Bank for International Settlements 1939–45 by John Lowen

(winner of the 2010 Threadneedle Literary Award)

Introduction (by Paul Tempest)

Born in Basle in 1930 with major input from the Bank of England, the Bank for International Settlements shouldered, as its first task, the need to sort out the fiasco of the massive reparations levied on Germany by the Allies at the end of the first World War. Within a decade, the BIS found itself on the horns of another major global dilemma. How do you continue to run the operations of an international bank and agency when some of your major shareholders are again at war with each other?

For some of the BIS international staff, this was, for themselves and their families, no less than a matter of life or death or, at best, incarceration in a concentration camp. Barely five miles away, German armed forces were preparing to strike and occupy Northern Switzerland and the Gestapo were known to have a black list of BIS undesirables supplied by a Nazi party-member on secondment from the Reichsbank. The response was a panic decision to move the whole BIS, lock, stock and barrel, to a remote mountain hotel in Central Switzerland as quickly as possible.

As the BIS recovered its nerve in its new temporary surroundings, it continued to publish its Annual Report based on its highly-regarded monthly and annual reviews of the European states and global outlook. The mandate was to preserve a high standard of accuracy without giving offence to either side. How, for example, do you assess the value of forced labour in Nazi Germany and the newly occupied countries of Europe? 'An unprecedented increase in the supply of skilled and unskilled labour in Germany', wrote the Swedish Economic Adviser to the BIS, 'has indeed, at low cost, given competitive advantage'. Such feats of diction and diplomacy earned Per Jacobsson promotion to become Chairman and Managing Director of the International Monetary Fund in Washington DC.

John Lowen's keynote article in the issue of Threadneedle, *of June 2010, based on recently released material from the BIS, explains how delicate this task became. By the closing stages of the War, the BIS faced the accumulated wrath of the Reichsbank and the Japanese, while a US resolution at the Bretton Woods conference insisted on closing the BIS down, once and for all. Only by a whisker and thanks to a co-ordinated filibuster by various European shareholders led by the Bank of England, did the BIS survive.*

John Lowen

The BIS in 1939–45

The BIS was founded in1930 under the Young Plan, as part of an attempt to resolve once and for all the contentious issue of Germany's World War I reparations. It collected and redistributed reparation payments (hence the 'settlements' featuring in the name of the Bank). From the outset, it was clear that senior central bankers – not least Montagu Norman (Governor 1920–44) – intended the BIS should be more than just a reparations bank. Hence it was given a broader statutory mission to 'promote the cooperation of central banks and to provide additional facilities for international financial operations ...', thereby fulfilling a longstanding idea to establish an international organization for central banks which had been frequently expressed since the 1880s.

The BIS soon carved out a role for itself as 'custodian' of the gold standard, and was at the forefront of the central banks' response to the financial crisis of 1931, providing technical advice and co-ordinating credits in support of the Austrian National Bank and the Reichsbank. These efforts have been usually dubbed too little too late, though, in the absence of a political will to embrace some degree of reparations forgiveness there was probably not much more the BIS and central banks could have done by themselves to stem Germany's financial meltdown, and by implication hinder the rise of National Socialism. A poignant reminder of the limits of central bank cooperation. The Bank survived the end of reparations in 1932, first by providing a discreet forum where central bank officials could exchange views in an informal and relaxed setting; and secondly, by developing its economic and monetary research activities.

An authoritative new book* devotes considerable attention to the much-criticised behaviour of the BIS during World War II. The authors have discovered no smoking gun. Indeed they begin on a positive note by highlighting a little known role of the Bank in assisting European central banks, apprehensive of the gathering war clouds, to move their gold to safe havens: between June 1938 and June 1940 the BIS was instrumental in shipping over 140 tonnes of gold for safekeeping to the United States.

In fact the most serious blemish on the Bank's reputation occurred before the outbreak of hostilities. The notorious Czechoslovak gold affair of 1939 is well related in this book. The authors are surely right to set it firmly within the context of appeasement. Even so it is difficult to acquit the Bank's management of political naivety and of acting with indecent haste. The decision to surrender a large part of Czechoslovak gold reserves to the Reichsbank did more to discredit the Bank than any of its wartime activities. In March 1939 as German troops were occupying Prague, a

**Central Bank Cooperation at the Bank for International Settlements* 1930-1973 by Gianni Toniolo, published by Cambridge University Press.

detachment entered the premises of the Czechoslovak National Bank and forced two directors at gunpoint to issue instructions to the BIS for the transfer of 23.1 tonnes of gold from the account of the Czechoslovak National Bank in the books of the BIS held at the Bank of England to the Reichsbank's gold account with the BIS also held at the Bank of England. The BIS soon executed the instructions, finding no grounds in Swiss law for declining them. The Reichsbank then proceeded to take full possession of the Czechoslovak gold by emptying its account with the BIS in London, in spite of British Government measures blocking all Czechoslovak assets in the UK. (The Bank of England insisted it could not know the ultimate owner of gold on BIS accounts in its books). After carefully planned location exchanges, the bullion in question was then transported from Brussels and Amsterdam to the Reichsbank's vaults in Berlin. The affair became a major embarrassment for the BIS and the Bank of England, especially when Churchill seized upon it to denounce the Chamberlain Government for negligence in failing to prevent the Nazis from building up their gold reserves.

BIS management at the time of the Czechoslovak gold affair found itself in an unenviable predicament. The BIS had after all been founded to promote international cooperation. In the prevailing climate of appeasement it is to some extent understandable that, isolated in neutral Switzerland, they should have hesitated to antagonise the powerful Reichsbank by declining to execute instructions which from a strictly formal point of view appeared unexceptional. Nevertheless it should have been clear to the BIS that the situation in Prague was highly irregular. After the German occupation of the rump of Czechoslovakia in defiance of the Munich agreements, appeasement lost its last shreds of credibility even in the eyes of such champions as Chamberlain and Lord Halifax. Against this background an international organization might have been expected to take a broader view of the circumstances rather than simply apply standard Swiss banking law. At the very least they could have delayed action pending a more thorough appraisal of the facts. Indeed, this was how the BIS subsequently proceeded when confronted with similar situations in the future. They did not have long to wait. For in June 1940 the Red Army, in implementation of the Molotov-Ribbentrop Pact, began to occupy the three Baltic states (Estonia, Latvia and Lithuania) as a prelude to their formal incorporation into the Soviet Union. In July the BIS received instructions from each of the Baltic central banks to make its gold held with the BIS available to the State Bank of the USSR. This time BIS management, smarting from the furore over the Czechoslovak gold sought an external opinion on international law and declined to execute the transfer instructions. It was just as well, since the Baltic states soon fell under German control as the Wehrmacht passed through on its way to Leningrad. There was now a precedent for not complying with new transfer instructions from the German-controlled Baltic central banks. In fact, the gold in question was held by the BIS for many years and finally placed at the free disposal of the Baltic states once they achieved independence from the Soviet Union.

Early into World War II, the central banks, with an eye to the future, came to a crucial decision to keep the BIS alive and active during the War rather than simply dormant. In December 1939 the BIS accordingly adopted a policy of strict neutrality which committed the Bank to avoid transactions to the advantage of one group of belligerents over another. However, not all the Bank's operations during the War can be squared with this self-imposed policy: in late 1941 for example, the BIS facilitated gold/escudo swaps between neutral Portugal and not-so neutral Vichy France. Various gold transfers on behalf of the Reichsbank to Hungary and Yugoslavia under the pretext of postal or railway business also look dubious and may have concealed war-related payments (many German troops were stationed in these countries). The victorious Allies came to regard all these operations with deep suspicion after the War.

Yet the activity of these years that was to cause most embarrassment to the Bank represented no breach of the neutrality policy but rather arose from tasks originally entrusted to the Bank under the Young Plan whereby the BIS had made direct investments in Germany, a well-intentioned initiative to support the Weimar economy. The Reichsbank continued to transfer interest payments on these investments during the War when they became the BIS's main source of income, leaving it vulnerable to Reichsbank pressure. Interest was payable in Swiss francs but in March 1940 the Reichsbank began to settle the payments in gold. Much of which, it later transpired, had been looted from the Dutch and Belgian central banks, a possibility to which BIS management was, admittedly, alerted at the time. After the War the gold in question was returned by the BIS to the Allied Tripartite Commission for the Restitution of Monetary Gold. More disturbingly, it now seems possible that some of this gold had in the smelting process been tainted by 'victim gold' looted from private citizens of countries under Nazi subjugation including inmates of concentration camps.

During the War the US administration regarded the BIS with growing misgiving as an institution subservient to German influence. They also considered the BIS implicated in the failure of inter-war economic policies and hence in some degree responsible for the Great Depression. These were the views of US Treasury Secretary Henry Morgenthau, and were shared by Harry Dexter White, another influential voice at the Treasury. The hostility of these men does much to explain the resolution passed at Bretton Woods calling for the dissolution of the BIS. Officially the establishment of the IMF and the World Bank was supposed to make the BIS redundant in the new global monetary order. Curiously, the resolution was put forward by a Norwegian delegate at the Conference. He must have been acting as a front for the Americans since the Norges Bank was a BIS member and bore no grudge against the Bank. The resolution was vigorously opposed by Keynes and officially revoked in 1948. By this time the BIS was well underway to reinventing itself again and demonstrating its usefulness within the Bretton Woods system.

The views expressed in this paper are those of the author and do not necessarily reflect those of the Bank for International Settlements.

John Lowen joined the Bank of England in 1981. After a secondment to the Bank for International Settlements, he joined its permanent staff in 1989. He was responsible for organising a public exhibition to commemorate the 75th anniversary of the BIS in 2005 and currently works in the BIS Banking Department.

Roger Barnes

Bishop Blougram Reflects on the BCCI Trial

(with apologies to Robert Browning)
(winner of the 2009 Threadneedle Literary Award)

It was a strange ending to it, you 'll recall –
Come Sir, sit here and take a glass of Chardonnay –
The large man bearded and blustering
Leading his lady acolyte out of the door
Of the grey courtroom, – home for how many days ?
Two hundred and fifty, did you say? They left the boy
To tidy up the debris, you remember.

Mind you, the beginning was as strange
Those thirty five years before in Karachi.
Tall, brooding, driven, infuriated
By nationalisation, he plans a bank
To liberate believers from the exclusion and
Patronising practices the West accords.
Shi'ite or Sunni you ask? Shi'ite, I believe,
Although we did not greatly understand
The difference in those days. Agha Hasan Abedi.
A name to conjure with, Sir – a man of vision.

A suspect vision though, you claim, flawed from the
start?
A touch of hindsight there perhaps you'll grant.
To fellow Muslims a prospect of dignity;
Nor any problem to convince a patron
As the hawks swooped on their prey and
The horsemen swirled in the desert hunting grounds
Of Abu Dhabi. Fit for Allah's purpose.

Not a bad time either to start as oil shock
Followed oil shock and wealth cascaded
Into the pockets of his chosen clients.
You want a house in Knightsbridge – or
Should it be Chelsea? Which is closer
To the best casino? Abedi will proffer
Reliable advice and send a clerk round
With the cash for your evening's sport.
And not the rich only – who else will back
A new business in Leicester spoken for
Only by an uncle in Lahore?
Seeds of disaster from the outset, you suggest?
The urge to grow and to show success
From growing? Dodgy shipping loans
And the risk of casting good money after bad?
The obsessive urge to start up in the States?

You are acute, Sir, but not as easy to be certain
Of disaster some five and twenty years ago.

Yet you would have been braver, you say,
More willing to volunteer to probe and press?
Sir, it is your privilege to say so – another
Glass of wine to mark your fortitude!
Yet probe and press they did year after year
And with the years the pressure rose.

So came the day of crisis when the Master fell;
Crippled by his heart, they took him off
To stare unseeing at Kashmiri peaks.
Time to press more firmly; a new co-operative push.
Time too for pressure from within; the Master's
Dominance deflates and worried men confide
Who had hitherto kept quiet. Answers come to
Questions that had been fudged before.

The carousel speeds up – at the Miami wedding
The sting is sprung; the First American deceit
Unravels; fumes stir in Washington and in New York
Moscow's jurors prowl;
The pit that is Gokal is slurried out.

Is there a future then when costs are summed?
Someone thinks so – part embarrassment perhaps,
Partly residual credence in what Abedi dreamed.
Do you think, Sir, that acceleration by itself
Can shatter dreams? It did so now – with what a mighty
bang!

Time for bewilderment and loss; phone lines
In Urdu and Bengali to explain the unexplainable.
Time too for blame and anger. Then the rolling out

Of scrutinies by wise or motivated men.
At last the aridity of 'principal place of business';
The frivolity of conspiracy constructions;
The mountains of paper and the painstaking
Recreation in four hours of incidents
That took four minutes in real life.

You have listened patiently. Sir, I thank you.
History will judge no doubt, but let it be
Less soulless than the past twelve years.

Roger Barnes joined the Bank in 1961 and retired in 1993, having been Head of Banking Supervision Division for the previous five years.

The BCCI case was brought against the Bank by the Liquidators of Bank of Credit and Commerce International which was closed down in the summer of 1991. Launched in 1993, their case claimed 'misfeasance in public office' by 22 Bank officials in the conduct of the supervision of BCCI. After considerable preliminary fencing, the case finally came to trial in January 2004 and collapsed in November 2005 when the plaintiffs suddenly withdrew from the action – having set records for the longest opening speech (80 days) and the longest opening reply (119 days) on the way. The trial judge declared that every allegation of dishonesty against any Bank official had been 'without foundation'.

Robert Browning (1812-89) had close links with the Bank. He was born in Camberwell and his father was a clerk at the Bank from 1803-53. According to William Sharp, Browning's leading biographer, his father was 'in the intervals of leisure which beset the best regulated clerk, addicted to making drawings of habitual visitors to the Bank of England'.

Bishop Blougram's Apology *is one of Browning's long blank verse poems (over 700 lines) in which a Church of England bishop muses to a journalist over a glass or two of wine as to whether and how he may have lost his faith.*

Peter Edgley

Bank-ese: A Forgotten Dialect?
(joint winner of the 2008 Threadneedle Literary Award)

Like most institutions, the Bank used to have its special expressions – not quite its own language, but certainly a special vocabulary. I wonder how much has survived in today's Bank?

Does anyone still get told to 'prick off the gones in the Kalamazoo', as I was on my first afternoon in a Stock Office? Two generations after the accounts were kept manually in Finsbury Circus and Regent Arcade House, the answer is 'almost certainly not'. Translated, it meant ' in the posh leather-bound, American-made ledger, cross off the stock accounts that are now empty'.*

Another expression I feel fairly certain will have dropped out of use by now is 'leaving someone a black man'. It means using the last line on a ledger page, but neglecting to rule up the next page ready for future use. I was introduced to it by the late Jimmy Axten of Accounts Office, who admitted he had no idea how it had arisen. Before the Thought Police come for me, I had better surmise that there must have been a long-forgotten clerk named Blackman who gave his name to this unhelpful habit.

Some of the language was purely archaic, such as the Drawing Office (withdrawing?), the Parlours, and the 18th century ranks such as Gatekeeper and Principal Clerk. Even Latin was occasionally pressed into service. 'Distringas' was the name for a particular kind of legal document on the Stock Side; as a Latinist, I was able to translate it at a trainees' quiz as 'See that you tie it up separately'. (I don't know why everyone laughed.)

Many words acquired a special Bank meaning, slightly different from that in common use. One such was 'quitter', which in fact was used in two quite separate contexts. In the

Establishment Department (Human Resources these days), a 'quitter' was someone who left the Bank voluntarily for another life – clearly a craven, even a disloyal fellow, in the eyes of those attuned to the forty-year career. In Exchange Control, it meant something equally pejorative but somewhat different – a British resident who, in wartime, had left the UK for a safer shore, taking his (or her) asset with him (or her).

Another such is 'plonker'. If you use it in the pub, it means a pompous ass; but in the Bank it meant getting an account or a reconciliation to balance at the first attempt (for some of us a relief as well as a source of satisfaction, in the days of manual accounting!).

Another specialised word which every reader must surely recognise is 'qualifying', in the sense of being trained for a particular task. This is the only Bank word I still find myself using habitually, as when I recently noticed that our youngest granddaughter was being 'qualified' on cake-making.

One phrase – again from the Stock Side – always made me think of Nelson's navy. When writing your History Sheet setting out the 'previous' (facts, not criminal record) and your recommendation, you always had to end with 'O.I.O.' – 'Otherwise in Order' – to show you hadn't overlooked any other error. In similar vein, sealed orders to an 18th century ship's captain about his next destination always began with the phrase 'Being in all respects ready for sea, you will proceed ...' (Knowing the Navy, they probably still do.) One is tempted to continue, but I can imagine the Editor reaching for his red pen.

Do any readers recall the expression 'House' (meaning 'the Bank') being in general use, other than among the Sports Club community? My impression is that it may have been more used before the Second World War than after.

**There was an incident in War Stock Office in October 1959, when a school-leaver, newly arrived in the Bank, was told to PRICK OFF. She burst into tears, excused herself and rushed out of the office. She never came back.*

As I See It – Building Bridges

Alan Watson
(joint winner of the 2008 Threadneedle Literary Prize)

When sorting out some papers recently, I came across an article which I had written for *The Old Lady* in 1969 in the 'As I See It' series.

What I wrote nearly forty years ago was the need for improved communications between people if we were to break down some of the barriers in human relations. I believe this to be even truer today, as we live in a society which has become increasingly complex. It is ironic that technological advances have facilitated communications as never before, but they are often used (or abused) in such a way as to avoid face to face conversations and meetings, for which I believe there is no satisfactory substitute.

Now that I have graduated to the generation of 'grumpy old men', I should be showing signs of increasing intolerance. I am sure I have as many Victor Meldrew moments as many others, as I fume at the papers or other news media, but when I analyse what raises my blood pressure, it is often rather petty matters such as a lack of care or pride by people who discard litter, park their cars inconsiderately or fail to show appreciation when they accept other people's help. I speak of these as petty, but while they might not be significant in themselves, they arise from a more fundamental selfishness which is disturbing. Also, I am saddened, rather than maddened, by so many people failing to value – or abusing – the freedom which we enjoy as a society, not recognising that it was so dearly bought by those who gave their lives for its preservation.

I have long held the view that if relationships – whether personal, business or community – are to develop satisfactorily, there must be shared values, similar attitudes and mutual trust. We need strong values more than ever if we are to succeed in developing a more harmonious and peaceful society. But that is not to say that those of us who can boast a longer British pedigree than some others should consider that we have the monopoly of wisdom or that our ways of thinking and doing things are sacrosanct. If we are to benefit from the values which others regard as important, there has to be a willingness to develop a dialogue and to listen; and to show a tolerance which seems to be sadly lacking in many people.

I was brought up to think of compromise as a sign of weakness, and perhaps it is if we see it as threatening our integrity, but a degree of compromise is essential in most marriages and families. If my wife and I had tried to impose the same strict moral standards on our teenage children as those to which we had been subjected, I doubt whether any of them would still be speaking to us. We were agreed that the priority was to keep the family intact and maintain loving relationships, even if that meant relaxing some standards in which we believed. We like to think that this worked, as they are all living satisfactory, moral and caring lives, and we all get on pretty well together.

I think it reasonable to suggest that those principles which we apply to our personal lives can often be applicable to broader relationships. It seems to me that we need a far greater tolerance in our community and a greater willingness to listen to others whose values might seem to be very different from ours, but who might have a good deal of worth to bring to our society. So often fear comes from ignorance, and if those of different backgrounds and faiths were only to listen to, and learn from, each other, we might reduce many of the tensions in our society.

It is often difficult to express such views without being misunderstood, as the Archbishop of Canterbury found when speaking of Sharia Law, but there is a dangerous tendency to make a knee-jerk reaction to headlines rather than make a considered response to what is said in its full context. So let me make it as clear as possible that I am not in any way suggesting that we should abandon whatever it is that we stand for, but rather that we think through what really matters to us and analyse how best that can be accomplished. We might well find that we can compromise without losing our integrity and that, in doing so, we shall gain more than we lose; build bridges rather than barriers; and will be able to move towards a more peaceful and harmonious society. It seems to me that any alternative is likely to be far worse.

First Impressions

Jeremy Morse

I joined the Bank in October 1964 from Glyn, Mills & Co, where I had had 11 years of excellent grounding in banking and the workings of the City. I was 35, young enough to be excited but old enough to understand and appreciate the change. So perhaps it is not surprising that the impressions I formed in my first months at Threadneedle Street still remain vivid.

Two things quickly made me feel at home. The Bank building, formidable as it is, was only a grander version of Glyns' head office in Lombard Street: both had been rebuilt by Herbert Baker in the 1930s. And the staff I met in my introductory tour of departments were remarkably alike in stamp and outlook to those I had known at Glyns. The managers had nearly all joined the Bank from school, usually grammar school, and had children who were going to university. I had expected to find them 'praisers of past times', but not a bit of it; they felt that during Cobbold's Governorship, the Bank had become a better place to work in than it was when they began – less hierarchical, but retaining enough order to be efficient.

The exception to this general pattern was at the top of the Bank where the select group who attended Governor's Books represented a notable variety of background, personality and talent. There were Bank men like Leslie O'Brien, Maurice Parsons and Jasper Hollom; market men like Roy Bridge; economists like Maurice Allen, John Fforde and Kit McMahon; former civil servants like Jasper Rootham and commercial bankers like the Governor, Rowley Cromer and myself.

My friends outside the Bank would ask me how my change of job was going. After a few months' experience I could give them a balance-sheet on the following lines:

A I was missing the profit motive. Times weren't easy, with a new Labour government and weak sterling and jittery markets; yet there was no obvious way of measuring how the Bank was doing. A commercial organisation in such conditions could point to its results and say 'We may not be doing very well, but at least we are doing better than some of our rivals'; but the Bank had no such comparators. However, the excitement I had lost on this score was partly made up by the excitement of defending the sterling exchange rate.

B I was also missing the customers, whose variety is the spice of the commercial banker's life. I remember O'Brien saying that when he came to retire it would be hard for him, after dealing with the big issues to work up an interest in boots or beer. Whereas I felt that boots and beer were the stuff of life to which the more theoretical big issues should be anchored.

C To balance these minuses, I quickly discovered a big plus, the centrality of the central bank. Poised between government and market, and well-informed about both, the Bank offered as central – and objective – a viewpoint as one could ask for. And later on when I got to go regularly to Basle, this central viewpoint extended to the international scene.

Finally, although there were the usual particular grouses and grumbles. Bank staff appeared generally satisfied with their pay and conditions. They had a job for forty years or until they were sixty; and with central banking not then so specialised, those who wanted a post-retirement job in the City had a good chance of finding one. Except at the top, they were paid a bit more than their commercial banking counterparts, an advantage they lost with the later introduction of incomes policies which were more strictly observed by the Bank than by the market. And the Bank itself was seen as holding a unique intermediary position, exemplified in the pleasing fiction that the Issue Department was in the public sector and the Banking Department in the private sector.

All in all, it was a good time to join the Bank.

Sir Jeremy Morse KCMG was Executive Director of the Bank of England in 1965-72, Chairman of Lloyds Bank in 1977-93 and Non-executive Director of the Bank of England in 1993-7.

Guy de Moubray

Two things happened to me on my first day at the Treasury at end-September 1948. I was passed a file. It concerned the negotiations regarding the outstanding Anglo-Dutch wartime debt, somewhere between £8 and £12 million pounds. Negotiations seemed not to have gone very far and there were clearly things which could be done. I was told to get on with it and settle the debt. I don't know whether such decision-making ability is innate or cultivated; but I do know that this experience – at 23 years old on my first day – strengthened it in me. I was later to see complete atrophy among some young graduates in the Bank of England, where such responsibility would not have been given to anyone under the age of about 45.

The second even more important thing that happened that day was that a beautiful girl put her head round the door. So that was the first time I saw Daphne Hazell, my future wife. It was Daphne who suggested my new career. She said that on her frequent visits to Germany she kept meeting very prosperous looking gentlemen from the Bank of England; why did I not at least think about it? I had visited the Bank once with the Belgian Financial Attache and been given tea served in a silver teapot by a pink coated messenger. So I agreed.

I was told I would have to go through the normal procedures and would have to be seen by a Selection Board. On this occasion the Chairman was Humphrey Mynors then a Director but later to be Deputy Governor. As I fear is often the case, I was not particularly humble at the meeting and began to interview them. I said that in the light of my experience at the Treasury the starting salary was quite inadequate – £360 a year was significantly less than I was earning at the Treasury (£400 a year). Humphrey Mynors put me in my place. 'Young man, you have a lot to unlearn!'

This was a significant remark; although the Bank as a whole was of a significantly lower calibre than the Treasury, Bank men looked down on the Treasury, who were seen as being too subservient to politicians, not sufficiently committed to sound finance and woefully ignorant of the workings of financial markets.

One of the most remarkable days in my life

It was a Friday in late October 1956. I had driven to the Bank from home in Pulborough, Sussex and parked my little car in Tokenhouse Yard at the back of the Bank. Anyone who knows the City today would be amazed that it was possible to park there. It is a tiny lane. Later that morning, the Chief Cashier, Leslie O'Brien asked to see me. He asked me if I knew Per Jacobsson. I told him I knew who he was and had met him briefly when a bag carrier to Basle. 'Well,' he said, pointing to the other side of the Garden Court, 'Jacobsson is in that room and he wants to see you now.'

Jacobsson had asked to see me because he was looking for someone from the Bank to be his Personal Assistant at the IMF in Washington DC to which he had just been appointed as the Chairman and Managing Director. As a Swede, he felt the need to have an Englishman to help him with his speeches. Through that week, the Bank had sent him three or four young men to interview, all of whom he had found quite hopeless. During this period he spoke to his daughter Moyra (Mrs Roger Bannister) and asked her if she knew of anybody bright in the Bank. She had been at the Ruskin School of Art when I had been up and knew that I was in the Bank and had heard, how I don't know, that I would probably be just what he was looking for. So he had asked for me by name. With great reluctance, the Bank allowed him to see me. Within a very few minutes, we knew that we would hit it off very well. He was particularly pleased that I had already completed an 18-month secondment to the IMF in 1953–4 and already knew all the people in it. So after about half-an-hour he confirmed that he would like me to go to Washington with him for about two years.

I went back to see O'Brien but he had already gone to lunch. I spoke to his secretary, Mrs Smith. We both agreed that nothing could be done about my appointment before the following Monday and that I might as well drive home to Sussex.

Hardly had I gone than the Governor asked to see me. The Bank gave the police and the AA a description of my car and the number plate and told them to stop me and turn me round. But I drove too fast for them and reached home just in time to see a police car racing up the drive. There was no sign of Daphne, then seven months pregnant, who had been much mystified by a message from the Bank that I might be very late on account of 'having to cross the pond'. I answered a call from the Bank: I was to proceed to the Governor's flat in Green Strreet, Mayfair, as fast as I could.

When I arrived, there was Cobbold pacing up and down in white tie and tails, with Lady Hermione in the car and Gale, the chauffeur standing patiently by. Cobbold took me by the arm and walked me up and down, telling me that it was his earnest wish that I should go to Washington with Jacobsson, that I should sail on the *Queen Mary* with Mr and Mrs Jacobsson in two weeks' time and that I should now go to the Kensington Palace Hotel where Jacobsson was expecting me for dinner.

Over the next few days, we organised all that needed to be done. The Bank made the booking on the *Queen Mary* and Cunard required us to sign an indemnity in case the unborn child came to any harm. We arranged to let our house and decided to take the dogs with us.

Guy de Moubray joined the Bank from the Treasury in 1950 and left in 1976 to become Adviser to the Governor of the Central Bank of Morocco. During a part of his period with the Bank, he was seconded to be personal assistant to Per Jacobsson, Chairman of the International Monetary Fund and later served as Deputy Chief of the Economic Intelligence Department and Chief of the Management Development Division in the Establishments Department. All these experiences are covered in detail in his 430-page autobiography entitled City of Human Memories, *published by The Memoir Club in 2005.*

Roger Stevenson

A far cry from being Adjutant at Royal Signals Headquarters in Catterick, I rejoined the Bank in January 1947 and spent a dull period of six months on the stock side, followed by two years in Overseas. Here the quarters were excellent; the quality of my colleagues was high, all keenly making their mark, but the hours were long because there was a strong reluctance on anybody's part to be the first to go home. While silence prevailed in the Office, there was plenty of opportunity to chat at coffee mid-morning, a pre-lunch snifter in a City pub, lunch itself in the Bank Club while tea was served at our desks by a liveried Office Messenger.

Roger Stevenson joined the Bank in 1939 and left in 1964 to take up a permanent appointment in the Bank for International Settlements in Basle where he and Gwen still reside. He has been an enthusiastic member of the Threadneedle Club since its inception in 1985 and has deposited the manuscript and tapes of his extensive memoirs in the new Threadneedle archive.

Mike Lees

'Play your cards right, Lees, and you should end up a four-figure man' said my careers master. I arrived on a cold December morning in 1957 to take up my position in the Consols Stock unit. By the end of that day, having been surrounded by a number of attractive young girls – bearing in mind a monastic existence at public school followed by two years with no prospects of eligible females while serving Her Majesty on National Service – and having had a good lunch for a shilling, I came to the end of the beginning a very contented man. However, four figures still seemed a distance away.

Mike Lees completed 33 years in the Bank, retiring in 1991.

Snapshots

Malcolm Gill

Meetings – A Question of Attitude

I remember seeing at a Management Course or an Awayday a film about meetings featuring John Cleese. As I recall it was mainly about how, and how not, to conduct meetings. But my experience in the financial institutions in which I worked is that there were also quite different attitudes to meetings.

In the Bank meetings were usually held in the room of the senior person, with the other participants assembled in a semi-circle around his (and it was 'his') desk. It was the same arrangement at Books with the Governor. (For Books with the Chief Cashier the others simply stood.) Actual meeting rooms were few and far between. These rather uncomfortable arrangements suggested that meetings were to be discouraged – and brief. As one veteran put it to me: 'In the Bank you either do as you are told, or you tell others.'

After a few years I went to the IMF as part of the UK Treasury Delegation. There I found a very different style. It was quite a small delegation but senior members (not including myself) had offices furnished with sofas and easy chairs. Meetings were held in this relaxed atmosphere. They probably lasted longer as a result.

Some years later I went to HM Treasury. Here any fairly senior official, such as I had then become, had a room equipped with table and chairs for meetings, as well as a desk. Meetings were great events. I remember holding a meeting where one participant apologised for coming tie-less – probably quite normal nowadays. He said he wore a tie only for meetings and kept them in his safe but the safe had jammed. Some meetings were more like university seminars. Getting a word in edgeways was like trying to emerge from a side road on to a busy dual carriageway.

The BIS was different again. Part of the BIS's role is to provide a home for meetings of central bankers and so it is hardly surprising that it is splendidly equipped with meeting rooms of different shapes and sizes, furnished to the highest BIS standard, with translation facilities, if needed, microphones, messengers and so on. Such refinements were not needed for internal BIS meetings but holding them in such grand surroundings almost made the most enervating discussion on a new computer project feel of global importance.

Whether these varied arrangements for meetings made any difference to the quality of the decision-taking is far from clear.

Malcolm Gill joined the Bank in 1957 and left in 1991. He was Chief Cashier from 1988 to 1991 after serving on secondment in the UK Treasury Delegation to the IMF from 1966 to 1968 and to HM Treasury from 1977 to 1980. He was Head of Banking Department in the Bank for International Settlements in Basle from 1991 to 1999.

Peter Longmuir

Official Duties with the Discount Houses

Part of the role of the Senior Manager, Money Markets, (formerly and perhaps better known as the Assistant Principal, Discount Office) was to call each morning on two or three Houses so as to have visited all 11 at least once every week. Often money discussions took place over a drink or two. Sometimes an invitation to stay for lunch followed, ending by 2.15 in case any borrowing from the Bank at 2.30 was needed.

- At Seccombe's the first drink of the day was coffee: here David Campion would clarify (for me) his 10 am conversations with Eddie George and Tony Coleby and once showed me a poem about the Discount Market penned by Andrew Crockett. Then began a round of certain Banks and Houses.
- At Smith St Aubyn my first lunch was a bit of a challenge. After two gin and tonics, I was invited to carve the beef! To this day I know not whether it was a test of a steady hand, or a custom reserved for Bank of England guests.
- At Clive Discount it was a great pleasure to talk with John Warr's guest, fellow England cricketer, Denis Compton, glass in hand, more than once.
- At Gerrard and National, a most sociable house, with David Clarke (Hilton's son) the only non-Etonian director, lunch was always most enjoyable as, after a brief discussion with Brian Williamson on the merits of 'disintermediation', conversation was invariably about sport, helped by fine wines. Their Chairman, Roger Gibbs, always accompanied me down in the lift, to point me back in the direction of the Bank, often donning his top hat minutes later, to go to seek funds.

Peter Longmuir joined the Bank in 1956 and retired in 1980. He was seconded from 1965 to 1966 to the East Caribbean Currency Authority where he met his wife-to-be.

Lawrence FT Smith

Highlights of Two Bag-Carriers

The arrival of the Governor's Rolls Royce to collect me from our tiny South East London home led to a certain amount of curtain-twitching on the part of our neighbours. And British European Airways' action in losing Roy Bridge's suitcase provided invaluable qualification that stood me in good stead when suffering the same indignity on my own later Bank travels. Being driven at high speed over icy roads and Basle tramlines by the wife of the resident Bank man in her Triumph Herald (never particularly stable even on dry, immaculate roads) will be remembered to my dying day (which, to my surprise, did not occur that night).

Then the Bank decided to send Judith, my wife, as bag carrier (in an act of extraordinarily modern thinking – which, however, did not extend to giving her equal pay in the five years she was on its books). Judith's visit to Basle, where she was introduced as 'one of the Bank's first lady economists', was, I heard, remembered long after the event.

One of the things I remembered about my own trip was the great weight of the Bag Carrier's brief case, which contained not only voluminous papers and newspapers for all, but also a heavy metal safe which held the Bank's code books, in case the unfortunate bag carrier was required to communicate secretly with the Bank. Judith also wondered whether, despite her own burden, she should offer to carry the briefcase of a non-executive Director who suffered from wartime injuries and walked with the aid of a stick so that he would have a hand free for the handrail on the aircraft steps. But he beat her to it – 'Can I carry your bag, Mrs Smith?' Judith felt that as she was (she hoped) blazing the trail for other women of the Bank, she could not let her gender down – even if the offer had come from an able-bodied member of the Governor's party, which it didn't.

Other Governors at the final lunch probably thought it would be inappropriate to discuss matters of high financial policy even with 'The Bank's lady economist'. But an alternative line of small talk emerged after Judith had selected the wine. The Governor of the Banque de France leaned across. 'That was an excellent choice. Why did you select that one?' Judith, seeing trouble ahead, paused before replying. 'Because I liked the picture on the label', she said quietly, bringing the conversation rapidly to an end.

Lawrence FT Smith (known also as Tim and, earlier in his Bank career, as Lefty) was appointed Personal Assistant to the Managing Director of the International Monetary Fund in Washington DC and Financial Counsellor in the British Embassy in Tokyo where, unknown to him at the time,the Japanese on the visiting cards supplied to him by the Embassy, boldly announced him as Deputy to the Chancellor of the Exchequer. He returned to the Bank to become the Overseas Adviser covering the Middle East. After retirement in 1997, he completed two IMF assignments as General Policy Adviser to the Palestine Monetary Authority and worked for the EU at the Central Bank of Egypt. Judith Smith worked from 1963 to 1968 in the Economic Intelligence and Overseas Departments.

Paul Tempest

Punctuality

Punctuality in the old Old Lady meant a nine-o'clock start with no excuses. Once the line was drawn – most often with ten minutes' grace – you were LATE. You had to explain yourself to the Principal, a black mark on the Ledger.

The system was not without mercy. Up to the early 1960s, before the Clean Air Act, dense winter fogs could hang around all day. With mechanical signalling and parts of the Railway still under steam, ice, snow and autumn leaves took a similar toll. If, say, you were held up by about an hour in the morning, it was considered sporting to try to get you away an hour earlier in the evening, so that, despite the discomforts of the journey, at least the family high tea or supper would not be disrupted. Those arriving at eleven might hope to get away by two, two hours earlier than normal. Indeed some never arrived at all. It was always said by employees of less enlightened City establishments that, in extreme weather conditions, bevies of Bank of England clerks struggling up from the Kent, Sussex and Hampshire coast could be seen alighting from their morning trains at about twelve in, say Croydon or Surbiton, or Orpington, to confer on the platform or to go for a beer and sandwich together before agreeing that it was time to take the next train home.

From Wilde Thyme *by Paul Tempest, published in the quarterly* The Old Lady of Threadneedle Street *between 1987 and 1990.*

Events

Gavin Gordon

Sterling and Watermarks

Sterling and *Watermark* are the names given to the narrowboats of the Bank of England Inland Waterways Society. *Sterling* was the first and there have been three *Watermarks*.

Navigational challenges are balanced by the tranquillity of the pace of travel, but there are also humorous moments to cherish. We once lost all of our tins of food into the dock as we were loading up. They slid gracefully into the deep. Not to be defeated, we borrowed a marine magnet from the boatyard and recaptured them. However, several of the waterlogged labels had become detached and from then on it was a lottery to discover if the evening meal would be graced by peaches or dog food.

We also witnessed some good-natured revenge. One boat was attempting to moor in a gap which required the next boat, already moored, to move up by about six feet. Its owner refused to co-operate for quite a while. When all had been achieved and calm restored, I mentioned to the new arrival that his neighbour had been quite rude. 'Ah', he said with a twinkle, 'I have a plan. I will put bread on his roof after dark and at dawn the ducks will stamp up and down over his head'. Sure enough, we were wakened at 5.00 am by a cacophony of quacking.

I once arrived direct from the City in a suit and with a briefcase in hand which gave the boatyard owner a terrible time – he thought it was a VAT inspection. Happy days!

For the Tercentenary celebrations in 1994, the BofE Inland Waterways Society decided to bring *Watermark* to London, partly as a recruiting drive. We were moored in Paddington and one evening had invited the Governors and Senior Officials to a champagne reception on the towpath.

Eddie George agreed to come but was heading off to a dinner and warned us he could not stay long. He duly arrived in his dinner jacket, looked round the boat and joined the group on the towpath for a glass of champagne. I spotted a drunk tottering along towards us, typical City worker in a sober suit. He joined the party and tried to pick up the thread of conversation. Not getting very far, he turned to Eddie and said 'Excuse me waiter, any chance of a drink?' A magic moment! It fell to me in due course to usher him politely on his way.

Gavin Gordon joined the Bank in 1960 and retired as the Manager of the Pensions, Loans and Welfare Department in 2000. He has been Secretary of the Threadneedle Club since 1990. All boats, past and present, belong to the BoE Inland Waterways Society and are financed by subscriptions and hire fees. The boat is moved every two or so years to give variety of location and tuition is available to novices.

Barry Hoffmann

A Great Centenary Victory In Kent

One of the fascinations of cricket is its uncertainty. There are occasions when, against all expectations, games are won. It doesn't happen very often, but it is exhilarating when it does. And invariably it is one incident that proves to be the catalyst or turning-point. Our Bank of England match in 2008 against Marden on our 86th annual Kent tour proved just such a game. An undistinguished batting performance on a blameless wicket saw us dismissed for 140 – not normally nearly enough against a team of Marden's calibre. To stand any chance, we needed to get their leading batsman out cheaply. A burly farmer, whose grandfather had opened the innings for Kent, he scores a hundred against us each year more often than not. He played the third ball he received from John Hodges a fraction too soon – probably deceived by his lack of pace – into the hands of Richard Down fielding, extremely bravely, at the shortest of short legs. General euphoria ensued. Thereafter with the aid and length of Phil Pitt's left-arm seamers – 6 for 55, ably supported by John Hodges 3 for 35 – wickets fell regularly and the day was eventually ours by 13 runs.

So instead of having to apologise to my opposite number for another uninspiring performance, I was able, with a broad smile, to shake his hand in front of the assembled company and thank him 'for giving us such a good game'. A moment to savour, as, to use a boxing metaphor, we had punched above our weight. It was also an excellent way to celebrate the Sports Club Centenary.

Barry Hoffmann joined the Bank in 1955 and retired in 1994. He contributed BESC sports reports to The Old Lady of Threadneedle Street *from 1960 until the magazine closed in 2007 and has organised the annual Kent Tour since 1968. His full report of the 2008 Kent Tour will be added to the Threadneedle Archive.*

Paul Tempest

A Master Forger Visits the Bank

In February 2009, a special visit was arranged for an ace forger of Bank of England notes to come into the Bank to meet the Chief Cashier, Andrew Bailey and to identify the product of his labours. Adolf Burger, who is 91, quickly spotted one of his own £5 notes. They were manufactured when he was an inmate of the Nazi concentration camp at Sachsenhausen and employed in creating fake £5, £10, £20 and £50 Bank of England notes to a total value of £135 million (£2 billion in today's money). The plan was to scatter these notes all over Britain and worldwide in the hope of destabilising the economy and destroying confidence in the financial markets. Knowing that these large denomination notes were generally folded up and pinned together in use in Britain, the Nazis gave instructions for pinholes to be added to all the notes. Burger took it upon himself to put one pinhole on each note straight through the image of Britannia. He knew that there was a London tradition of never defacing Britannia and hoped that no-one in Germany and someone in England would spot this oddity as a warning of forgery. Before leaving the Bank, Burger thanked Andrew Bailey and assured him that he had no intention of renewing his interest in banknote forgery.

In the early sixties in the Chief Cashier's Office, we were taking in every week several large packets or boxes of white Bank of England fivers and higher denominations sent to us direct by central banks in both western and eastern Europe. It was part of my job to ensure that they were properly logged and transferred to the Issue Office for detailed acknowledgement, inspection and follow-up. They were, almost without exception, the Nazi forgeries manufactured in Sachsenhausen during the War, many of which had been secretly deposited in sealed waterproof boxes at the bottom of Bavarian or Austrian lakes and subsequently recovered on profitable late-night fishing expeditions, presumably by the people who had put them there. It transpired that the boxes and packets were then split up and offered for sale by market traders and dubious travel agents and foreign exchange dealers all over the continent. The Issue Office had no difficulty at all in identifying these notes as forgeries.

The question in my mind was why Adolf Burger had waited over 60 years until the age of 91 to come to the Bank of England and what had triggered his decision to come. A little research quickly provided the answer. He had come to say thank-you to the Bank of England for saving his life and, on behalf of his fellow inmates, now almost all departed this life.

A book by and a film about Burger were in preparation. They mention the Gestapo doubting whether the forgeries were good enough and, as a result, sending someone to a Zurich bank with a bundle of the forged Bank of England notes, saying that he thought they might be counterfeit and asking for reassurance. When he returned to collect the notes, he was given certification from the Bank of England that the notes were genuine. Production of forgeries of Bank of England and US notes continued unabated at

Sachsenhausen until close to the end of the War.

As a member of a cosseted cadre of concentration camp inmates, all selected as specialists in security printing, Burger would have known for certain that their notes would never stand up to certification by the Bank of England. Also he would have known throughout that, if the Nazis lost faith in the forgeries, the members of the cadre would either have been executed immediately as a security risk or turned out into the main camp where resentment of their collaboration would have given them little chance of survival. After the War, Burger is unlikely to have pursued the matter in case any publicity prompted neo- or anti-Nazi reprisals or aroused the interest of the mafia gangs handling the forgeries.

A little ingenuity, a small forgery by persons unknown in the name of the Bank of England, might therefore have saved quite a number of lives.

A Murderous Attack in the Bank

In 1903, Kenneth Grahame was accosted in his room by a man who pulled a revolver from a roll of papers and fired. Thanks to the quick-witted duty Messenger, the assailant was quickly disabled with a fire-hose.

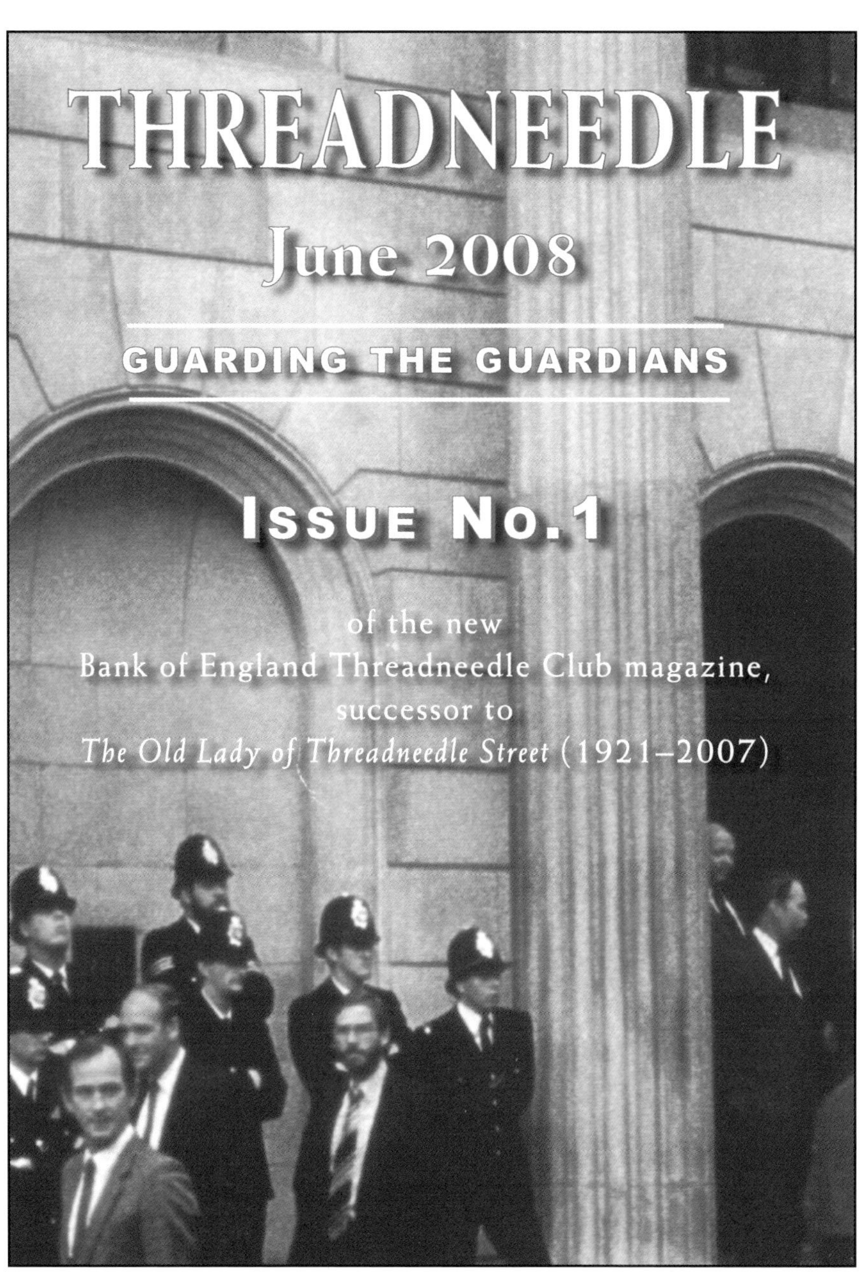
THREADNEEDLE
June 2008
GUARDING THE GUARDIANS
ISSUE No.1
of the new
Bank of England Threadneedle Club magazine,
successor to
The Old Lady of Threadneedle Street (1921–2007)

THREADNEEDLE
June 2009
A CALM AND STEADFAST HEART
ISSUE NO.2
of the new
Bank of England Threadneedle Club magazine,
successor to
The Old Lady of Threadneedle Street (1921–2007)

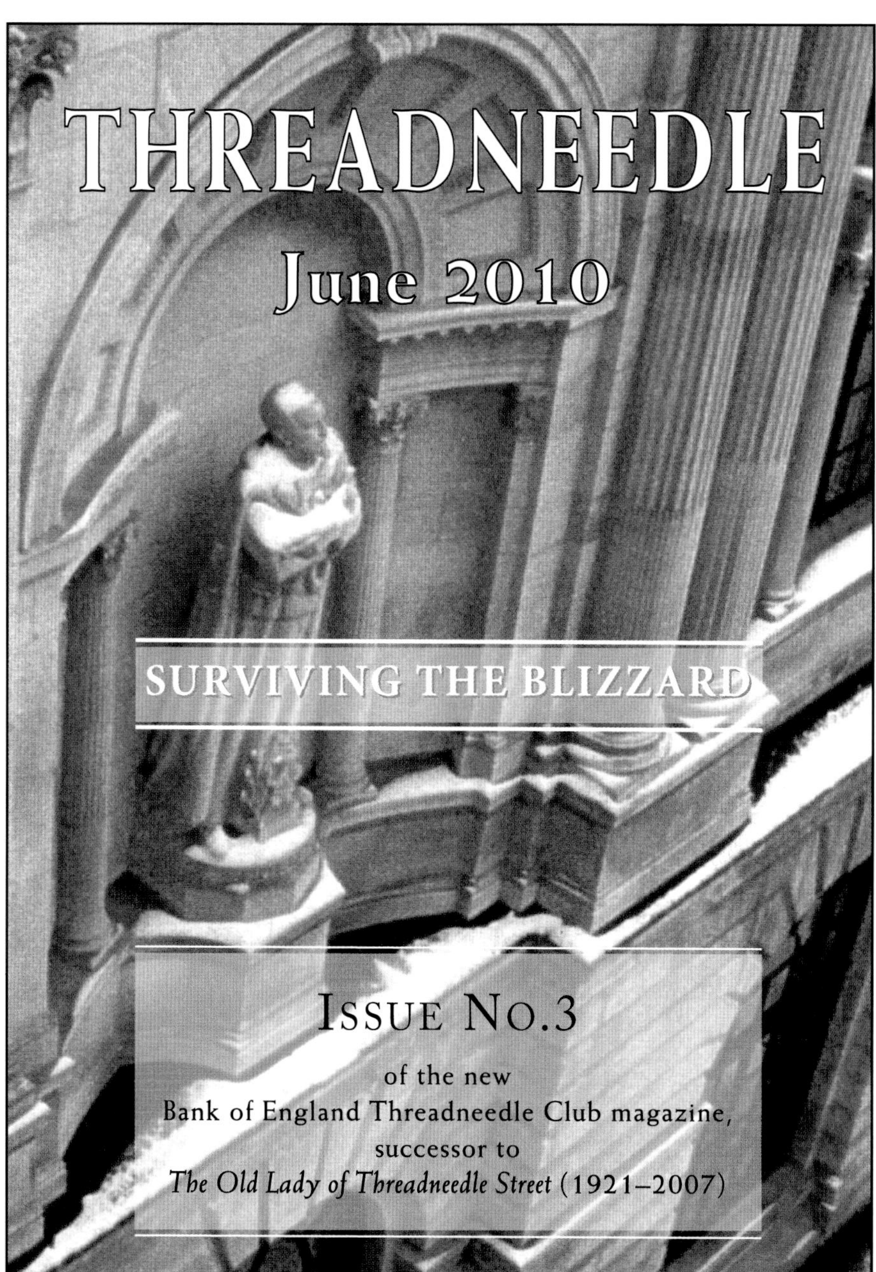
THREADNEEDLE
June 2010
SURVIVING THE BLIZZARD
ISSUE NO.3
of the new
Bank of England Threadneedle Club magazine,
successor to
The Old Lady of Threadneedle Street (1921–2007)

2007 – You Are New to the Bank …

Robert Butt
from *The Old Lady of Threadneedle Street,* June 2007

You are new to the Bank, the Principal said,
So welcome and please take a seat.
And I'll try to explain just in case you've not read
What we do here in Threadneedle Street.

We balance the books of the nation, you know.
Not a task for the feeble or faint.
And the language we use to assist the cash flow
May strike you as odd, not to say, quaint.

It is all very well for the world and his wife
To spend like there'll be no tomorrow.
Just to hang on to their standard of life,
But we have to pay back what they borrow.

We were hopeful of PRUNING THE THICKET, you see,
But the exercise drove us to tears,
We were going to do it today, after tea,
Only someone had stolen the shears.

So remember when things start to prickle and irk
And you're feeling a trifle distraught,
There are many less interesting places of work,
Than THE LENDER OF LAST RESORT.

JAMES GILLRAY (1757–1815) and THE BANK OF ENGLAND

James Gillray's career as a pioneer caricaturist and inventor-engraver spanned the Napoleonic Wars, a period of great political tumult and anxiety. The persistent threat of a French invasion and the fraught government financing of the British naval and military effort brought the Bank of England into the forefront of public attention as repeated demands by the Government for large quantities of gold to arm and equip and pay the troops and sailors quickly stretched resources and depleted reserves of gold and silver. The City was in ferment as each squeeze diminished the resources and increased the risks of the merchants and bankers. Finally, In February 1797, the Bank of England had run down its reserves to such an extent that it was obliged to suspend payment of its notes in gold. For the first time, the Bank was obliged to issue low denomination notes of £1 and £2.

Gillray was particularly successful in satirising the extremes of political life – from the English would-be rebels taking their cue from French revolution of 1789 to the indolent and absent aristocracy and other ruthless landlords who inflicted misery and near famine on their tenants in both city and countryside. By 1811, Gillray had trodden on too many toes and suffered the inevitable reactions of those he had pilloried – he was declared insane and spent the last four years of his life confined to his room.

HOW THE GOVERNMENT TREATS THE CITIZENS

A March to the Bank, 1787

After the Bank of England had been attacked by the Gordon rioters in 1780, the Government decreed that a detachment of soldiers would protect the Bank each night. This practice persisted until 1973. The Bank Picquet quickly established a tradition of marching from their barracks to the Bank without ever halting. Gillray captures some of the resentment of City folk accustomed to moving easily and peacefully along the pavements and across the roads.

THE UNSUBTLE ART OF TURNING GOLD INTO PAPER

King Midas Turns Gold into Paper, 1797

The King is clearly labelled Bank of England. Here Gillray pillories the immediately recognisable Prime Minister, William Pitt the Younger, as the direct opposite to Midas who had the power to change all he touched into gold .

POOR JOHN BULL FOBBED OFF WITH BANK NOTES

Bank Notes ... Ah Poor John Bull, 1797

John Bull, representing the British public is in the Bank of England being duped into accepting paper money in place of gold. Clearly recognisable as the Prime Minister, William Pitt the Younger, the clerk is offering the notes politely while the two companions portrayed accurately as Charles James Fox and RB Sheridan representing the Whig Opposition are protesting and shouting "The Devil! The Devil!"

A TASTY DISH FOR THE FRENCH

A Feast for Napoleon, 1803

Napoleon is portrayed sitting down to a gargantuan dinner. Directly in front of him is a large round cream cake marked BANK OF ENGLAND. Napoleon had claimed that all he needed to be in possession of London, Parliament and the Bank of England was three days of fog.

POLITICAL RAVISHMENT – THE OLD LADY IN DANGER

Political Ravishment or The Old Lady of Threadneedle Street in Danger, 1797
This is the first known reference in print to the Bank of England as The Old Lady of Threadneedle Street. The Old Lady dressed in paper money is sitting on the locked gold and treasure chest marked prominently BANK OF ENGLAND. She is resisting the embrace and kisses of William Pitt, the Prime Minister, shouting loudly 'Murder! Murder! Rape! Murder! Oh you Villain! ... Ruin! Ruin! Ruin!' His hand is deep in the pocket of her dress, presumably hunting for gold coins.

The captions to the Gillray cartoons draw extensively on a pamphlet by John Keyworth, Curator of the Bank of England, published by the Bank of England Museum entitled *Amusing, Shocking, Informing: The Bank of England's Cartoons and Caricatures.*

PART ELEVEN

The Best is Yet to Come

Sir David Walker

at the 25th Annual Dinner of the Threadneedle Club held in Trinity House, London on 18 October 2010

The transfer of power to the Bank that is now in prospect is probably as significant a development in the life of the Old Lady as anything that happened over the past 100 years. In that comparison I include all the exigencies and industrial activities of the 1920s and 1930s, the exchange and many other controls during the Second World War, nationalisation and then the radically new monetary policies and independence in the 1990s. So we, two former Chancellors,[1] and a large group of alumni and friends of the Old Lady, have a keen interest in what is currently in train. It is not only significant for the Old Lady but, of course, much more widely for the City, for our country and indeed for the international financial system in which London plays a critical role. I want to make some observations on the challenge as well as the opportunity for the Bank in this complex situation. But my refresher course on the Bank's history and reflection on how the Old Lady got to where

---

1 Baron Howe of Aberavon, Chancellor of the Exchequer 1979–83 and Lord Lawson of Blaby, Chancellor of the Exchequer 1983–9.

she now is led me into some unexpected byways that I thought I might share with you very briefly, acknowledging my debt to Richard Sayers.[2] So here goes.

Early in the 20th century the then Governor thought the Bank was 'well-served by aloofness from higher education' (this related to a proposal to recruit graduates) and, a little earlier, a Miss Hogarth, the first Superintendent of Women Clerks, had secured a First at Oxford. During her 11-year stint at the Bank, she was apparently offered and turned down the headships of Girton, Cheltenham Ladies and Royal Holloway Colleges. Despite her evident merit, the Bank continued to believe that 'men alone could be employed in work requiring intelligence and education'. Even so, Miss Hogarth must have found work at the Bank congenial despite being designated, to the end, as a clerk.

But the Bank was more enlightened in other matters and, in 1907, in concern to provide sports facilities for staff (though I am sure with thought only for the men) the Court approved the purchase of the land at Roehampton for £15,000. On the matter of real estate, perhaps few of us were aware (I was certainly not) that the total cost of construction of the present Bank, completed in 1941, was £5.3 million. This was more than the original estimate of some £4 million because of the need to provide more accommodation for women clerks and more technology. But this was after a saving of £200,000 because the Wallbrook, whose course ran under the Bank, was in the event found to be dry, and did not need to be drained.

Let me highlight a couple of other gobbets. The first was the extraordinary clash between Cunliffe as Governor and successive Chancellors of the Exchequer (McKenna and Bonar Law) at a critical phase during the First World War when the Governor sought to insist that he dealt only with

---

2 Professor RS Sayers, author of *The Bank of England 1891-1944* published in 3 volumes by Cambridge University Press in 1976.

the Prime Minister; declined to sign a letter acknowledging the overriding responsibility of the Chancellor in relation to the national interest in wartime; and pressed for the dismissal of Keynes, who was then serving as an adviser at the Treasury. The then Deputy Governor's finest hour was in getting Cunliffe to behave less intemperately and, in the event, Cunliffe was effectively forced out of the Governorship.[3]

The second gobbet relates to the Bank's attitude to the press which has always been prudently cautious but was, for a long time, effectively hostile. As what it regarded as a significant policy departure, the Court decided in 1931 that a senior official might contribute, though only over his own name, articles in *The Old Lady* (that was, of course, the in-house precursor of the *Threadneedle*) 'confined to questions of fact and policy that were no longer urgent and to statements that would not hamper the freedom of the Bank'. And, extraordinarily, the first press conference given by any Governor, in 1930, was on the Bank's industrial policy, with no reference whatsoever made to monetary policy.

Congenial as it may be to disinter such anecdotes from the past, I want to move to the present and immediate future, focussing on the huge new responsibilities about to be brought, in some degree, brought back, to the Bank. Of course I have in mind the Bank's new financial policy and regulatory role rather than monetary policy, though there could on occasion be some degree of tension between them.

This is neither the time nor place for a review of all the inadequacies of both public and private sector policies and activities that contributed to the recent crisis, and simple generalisation is in any event always potentially misleading. But clearly much of what went wrong was in the end down to

---

3 See Part Six, page 54.

major failures of judgement on the part of both supervisors and bank boards. Which leads me to recall Governor Gordon Richardson's adage that 'Good judgement comes from experience, but the trouble in banking is that most relevant experience comes from earlier bad judgement'. There was certainly an abundance of it in the period before this recent crisis.

With great distinction and success the Bank has built an analytical capability in respect of monetary policy which is widely and rightly regarded as second to none in the world. The need now is to build a similar capability, which did not exist in either the Bank or the FSA, in respect of prudential and macro-prudential supervision, assembling all the relevant data in a timely way; deploying the best analysis; and then exercising the best judgement, drawing on all relevant experience. If we examine the style and content of regulation of banks over the last couple of decades, it is now easy to see how the role for such judgement was crowded out. Part of the problem was the greatly increased reliance placed on new financial theory which generated a lot of insightful mathematical analysis and equipped bankers and regulators with some powerful tools for thinking about their business. But it also seemed to cause a lot of bankers to rely excessively on the output of their models, sanctified by the regulators, and effectively to stop thinking about their business. This analytical capability was not, in contrast, applied to liquidity risk because funding did not seem to be much of a problem given the newly-emergent huge and very liquid markets. Nobody gave much thought to it.

And a particular and serious further problem arose as a result of the new regulatory architecture created in 1997. The FSA was, I have to say in my view rightly at the time, charged with regulating every kind of financial institution, so that it became the market conduct and consumer protection regulator as well as prudential supervisor. But market conduct and consumer protection involve checking for compliance with rules and, as one colleague aptly described it, this is 'lawyerly' rather than 'bankerly' activity. The result has been that the hard-edged, rule-based culture of market conduct and consumer protection came to eclipse the thoughtful, intuitive culture that is at the heart of successful prudential banking supervision. And all this in circumstances in which banks were making handsome profits; when the UK and world economy seemed to be performing very well; and when widely accepted modern financial theories were telling us that markets are inherently self-correcting, and could thus safely be left on autopilot. We can now see, with 20:20 hindsight, that this relaxed view was widely shared by both bank boards and their regulators, with disastrous consequences.

I do not propose to spoil dinner in this lovely Hall by dilating any further on what went wrong. The main elements of the story are familiar, and the challenge now is to put arrangements in place that minimise the risk of any repetition. The new arrangements proposed by the Treasury in their June consultation document, involving detachment of conduct of business regulation from prudential supervision; the return of institutional supervision of banks to Threadneedle Street; and assignment to the Bank of a statute-based financial policy responsibility potentially offer the best way forward. But much will depend on implementation, and I have some concern at the scale of the transfer of power and authority to the Old Lady, with greatly enhanced power inevitably complemented by similarly enhanced vulnerability.

In this context I attach particular importance to appropriate internal governance mechanisms to ensure that there is the right behavioural dynamic between the independent or non-executive members of both the Court and of the new Financial Policy Committee that is to be established. One starkly clear lesson from my corporate governance review completed in 2009 is the importance of the possibility and indeed normalcy of effective challenge to the executive by the non-executive in the boardroom environment. In most of the problem bank situations, such challenge was ineffective or largely absent, and unchallenged strategies devised and implemented by chief executives led to catastrophe. My analysis and recommendations have been criticised as undermining the role of the chief executive. But that reflects misunderstanding of the right sequence. The chief executive should be at the beginning and end of the decision-taking process, proposing strategy to the board at the outset and, after a process of appropriate challenge and, if necessary, modification, should be fully empowered by the board to execute the agreed strategy. What was missing in bank boards was the critical intermediate process between executive proposal and execution.

The most careful reflection is now needed on how this hard experience in bank boardrooms bears on the functioning of these now greatly more significant decision-taking responsibilities of the Old Lady. Without this, the Bank would in my view be in a dangerous position of over-mighty power which can be only partly mitigated or balanced by the arrangements being proposed for enhanced public accountability. But if appropriate internal governance structures are indeed put in place as I would hope and expect, I would say for the Old Lady, despite her immense record of achievement in the past, that the 'best is yet to come'.

Sir David Walker has been Chairman of Morgan Stanley International since 2004. He joined the Bank of England from HM Treasury in 1977 as Adviser, then Chief of the Economic Intelligence Department and as Director in 1982-93.

PART TWELVE

Lessons from the Banking Crisis

Mervyn King

Extracts from The Second Bagehot Lecture by Mervyn King, Governor of the Bank of England at the Buttonwood Gathering in New York City on 25 October 2010. The Lecture was titled 'Banking from Bagehot to Basel and Back Again' and is available in full on request from The Bank of England Press Office, London EC2 R 8AH. The Lecture also covered the recent experience of the United States, aspects of banking theory and remarks on other countries. It also contained a full list of references and further statistics covering commercial banks in the UK and United States and comparisons of senior unsecured debt and senior CDS premia for large UK and US commercial banks up to August 2010 (not included here).

Introduction

Walter Bagehot was a brilliant observer and writer on contemporary economic and financial matters. In his remarkable book *Lombard Street*, Bagehot brought together his own observations with the analysis of earlier thinkers such as Henry Thornton to provide a critique of central banking as practised by the Bank of England and a manifesto for how central banks could handle financial crises in future by acting as a lender of last resort. The present financial crisis dwarfs any of those witnessed by Bagehot. What lessons can we draw from recent and current experience to update Bagehot's vision of finance and central banking?

Surely the most important lesson from the financial crisis is the importance of a resilient and robust banking system. The countries most affected by the banking crisis have experienced the worst economic crisis since the 1930s. Output is somewhere between 5 percent and 10 percent below where it would have been had there not been a crisis. Unemployment is up, businesses have closed, and the direct and indirect costs to the taxpayer have resulted in fiscal deficits in several countries of over 10 percent of GDP – the largest peacetime deficits ever.

At the heart of this crisis was the expansion and subsequent contraction of the balance sheet of the banking system. Other parts of the financial system in general functioned normally. And we saw in 1987 and again in the early 2000s, that a sharp fall in equity values did not cause the same damage as did the banking crisis. Equity markets provide a natural safety valve, and when they suffer sharp falls, economic policy can respond. But when the banking system failed in September 2008, not even massive injections of both liquidity and capital by the state could prevent a devastating collapse of confidence and output around the world. So it is imperative that we find an answer to the question of how to make our banking system more stable.

As Bagehot knew only too well, banking crises are endemic to the market economy that has evolved since the Industrial Revolution. The words 'banking' and 'crises' are natural bedfellows. If love and marriage go together like a horse and carriage, then banking and crisis go together like Oxford and the Isis, intertwined for as long as anyone can remember. Unfortunately, such crises are occurring more frequently and on an ever larger scale. Why?

The Practice of Banking

For almost a century after Bagehot wrote *Lombard Street*, the size of the banking sector in the UK, relative to GDP, was broadly stable at around 50 percent. But, over the past fifty years, bank balance sheets have grown so fast that today they are over five times annual GDP. The size of the US banking industry has grown from around 20 percent in Bagehot's time to around 100 percent of GDP today. And, until recently, the true scale of balance sheets was understated by these figures because banks were allowed to put exposures to entities such as special purpose vehicles off balance sheet.

Surprisingly, such an extraordinary rate of expansion has been accompanied by increasing concentration: the largest institutions have expanded the most. The asset holdings of the top ten banks in the UK amount to over 450 percent of GDP, with RBS, Barclays and HSBC each individually having assets in excess of UK GDP. In the US, the top ten banks amount to over 60 percent of GDP, six times larger than the top ten fifty years ago. Bank of America today accounts for the same proportion of the US banking system as all of the top 10 banks put together in 1960.

While banks' balance sheets have exploded, so have the risks associated with those balance sheets. Bagehot would have been used to banks with leverage ratios (total assets, or liabilities, to capital) of around six to one. But capital ratios have declined and leverage has risen. Immediately prior to the crisis, leverage in the banking system of the industrialised world had increased to astronomical levels. Simple leverage ratios of close to 50 or more could be found in the US, UK, and the continent of Europe, driven in part by the expansion of trading books.

And banks resorted to using more short-term, wholesale funding. The average maturity of wholesale funding issued by banks has declined by two thirds in the UK and by around three quarters in the US over the past thirty years – at the same time as reliance on wholesale funding has increased.

As a result, they have run a higher degree of maturity mismatch between their long-dated assets and short-term funding. To cap it all, they held a lower proportion of liquid assets on their balance sheets, so they were more exposed if some of the short-term funding dried up. In less than fifty years, the share of highly liquid assets that UK banks hold has declined from around a third of their assets to less than 2 percent last year (Bank of England 2009). Banks tested the limits of where the risk-return trade-off was located, in all parts of their operations. As John Kay wrote about his experience on the board of HBoS, the problems began 'on the day it was decided that treasury should be a profit centre in its own right rather than an ancillary activity' (Kay 2008).

Moreover, the size of the balance sheet is no longer limited by the scale of opportunities to lend to companies or individuals in the real economy. So-called 'financial engineering' allows banks to manufacture additional assets without limit. And in the run-up to the crisis, they were aided and abetted in this endeavour by a host of vehicles and funds in the so-called shadow banking system, which in the US grew in gross terms to be larger than the traditional banking sector. This shadow banking system, as well as holding securitised debt and a host of manufactured – or 'synthetic' – exposures was also a significant source of funding for the conventional banking system. Money market funds and other similar entities had call liabilities totalling over $7 trillion. And they on-lent very significant amounts to banks, both directly and indirectly via chains of transactions.

This has had two consequences. First, the financial system has become enormously more interconnected. This means that promoting stability of the system as a whole using a regime of regulation of individual institutions is much less likely to be successful than hitherto. Maturity mismatch can grow through chains of transactions – without any significant amount being located in any one institution – a risk described many years ago by Martin Hellwig (Hellwig

1995). Second, although many of these positions net out when the financial system is seen as a whole, gross balance sheets are not restricted by the scale of the real economy and so banks were able to expand at a remarkable pace. So when the crisis began in 2007, uncertainty about where losses would ultimately fall led confidence in banks to seep away. This was obvious through the crisis. Almost no institution was immune from suspicion.

For most banks the spreads on their senior unsecured debt had more than trebled in October 2008 relative to their levels at the start of 2007. Similarly, credit default swap premia – the cost of insuring a bank's debt – shot up. All banks, irrespective of the precise nature of their business and balance sheet, were tarred with the same brush. Moreover spreads and CDS premia remain elevated today – almost universally, large UK and US banks face much higher borrowing charges compared to risk-free rates, and are seen as riskier entities, than prior to the crisis. The size, concentration and riskiness of banks have increased in an extraordinary fashion and would be unrecognisable to Bagehot. Higher reported rates of return on equity were superficial hallmarks of success. These higher rates of return were required by, and a consequence of, the change in the pattern of banks' funding with increased leverage and more short-term funding. They did not represent a significant improvement in the overall rate of return on assets. Not merely were banks' own reported profits exaggerating the contribution of the financial sector to the economy, so were the national accounts.

Moreover, a financial sector that takes on risk with the implicit support of the taxpayer can generate measured value added that reflects not genuine risk-bearing but the upside profits from the implicit subsidy. And even without an implicit subsidy the return to risk-bearing can be mis-measured. It is widely understood that an insurance company should not count as profits the receipt of premia on an insurance policy that will pay out only when a low-frequency event occurs at some point in the future. But part of the value added of the financial sector prior to the crisis reflected temporary profits from taking risk and it was only after September 2008 that much of that so-called economic activity resulted in enormous reported losses by banks.

It is possible to make a very rough estimate of the possible size of this distortion in the reported financial sector output data. If we assume that true labour and capital productivity in the financial services industry grew in line with that in the wider economy in the 10 years prior to the crisis, then, given the inputs of capital and labour over that period, the official estimate might have overstated UK financial sector value added by almost £30 billion up to 2007 – around half of the growth in the official measure. The impact of this adjustment on overall GDP is likely to be relatively small because much of the output of the financial sector is treated as intermediate inputs to other sectors in the economy. Such an estimate is supported by the finding of my Bank of England colleagues that the increase in rates of return on equity earned by banks were accounted for almost entirely by an increase in leverage, capital gains on assets in trading books and the reported profits on contracts that produced losses only after the crisis occurred. And it is consistent with the estimates calculated by Colangelo and Inklaar (2010) for the euro area. They found that around 40 percent of measured financial sector value added probably captured compensation for bearing risk.

The Theory of Banking

Why are banks so risky? The starting point is that banks make heavy use of short-term debt. Short-term debt holders can always run if they start to have doubts about an institution. Equity holders and long-term debt holders cannot cut and run so easily.

Not only are banks' assets risky, but banks are highly leveraged institutions. This leaves them heavily exposed – with very high debt-equity ratios, small movements in asset valuations are enough to wipe out their equity and leave banks insolvent. That means the distinction between illiquidity and solvency can be difficult in practice – the difference in timing might be just a few days. If a crisis is in fact one of insolvency, brought on by excessive leverage and risk, then central bank liquidity provision cannot provide the answer. Central banks can offer liquidity insurance only to solvent institutions or as a bridge to a more permanent solution.

It is this structure, in which risky long-term assets are funded by short-term deposits, that makes banks so hazardous. Yet many treat loans to banks as if they were riskless. In isolation, this would be akin to a belief in alchemy – risk-free deposits can never be supported by long-term risky investments in isolation. To work, financial alchemy requires the implicit support of the taxpayer.

When all the functions of the financial system are heavily interconnected, any problems that arise can end up playing havoc with services vital to the functioning of the economy – the payments system, the services of money and the provision of working capital to industry. If such services are materially threatened, governments will never be able to sit idly by. Institutions supplying such services are quite simply too important to fail. Everyone knows it. So, highly risky banking institutions enjoy implicit public sector support. In turn, public support incentivises banks to take on yet more risk, knowing that, if things go well, they will reap the rewards while the public sector will foot the bill if things go wrong. Greater risk begets greater size, most probably greater importance to the functioning of the economy, higher implicit public subsidies, and hence yet larger incentives to take risk – described by Martin Wolf as the 'financial doomsday machine'.

The failure in the crisis was not one of intellectual imagination or economic science to understand these issues. Economists recognised that distorted incentives, whether arising from implicit public subsidies, asymmetric information or a host of other imperfections, will cause a market-based outcome to be sub-optimal from the perspective of society.

The real failure was a lapse into hubris – we came to believe that crises created by massive maturity transformation were problems that no longer applied to modern banking, that they belonged to an era in which people wore whiskers and top hats. There was an inability to see through the veil of modern finance to the fact that the balance sheets of too many banks were an accident waiting to happen, with levels of leverage on a scale that could not resist even the slightest tremor to confidence about the uncertain value of bank assets. For all the clever innovation in the financial system, its Achilles heel was, and remains, simply the extraordinary – indeed absurd – levels of leverage represented by a heavy reliance on short-term debt.

What does reduce the cost of capital is the ability to borrow short to lend long. But the scale of maturity transformation undertaken today produces private benefits and social costs. We have seen from the experience of first Iceland, and now Ireland, the results that can follow from allowing a banking system to become too large relative to national output without having first solved the 'too important to fail' problem.

Finding a Solution

Many remedies for reducing the riskiness of our financial system have been proposed, ranging from higher capital requirements on banks to functional separation and other more radical ideas. The guiding principle of any change should be to ensure that the costs of maturity transformation

– the costs of periodic financial crises – fall on those who enjoy the benefits of maturity transformation – the reduced cost of financial intermediation. All proposals should be evaluated by this simple criterion.

The first, and most obvious, response to the divergence between private benefits and social costs is the imposition of a permanent tax on the activity of maturity transformation to 'internalise the externalities'. Such a tax, or levy, has been discussed by the G7, and introduced in the UK. The principle that the 'polluter pays' for the costs they impose on others is an old one, going back at least to Pigou in the 1920s. The main practical problem is to calibrate the costs to maturity transformation. The loss of world output from the financial crisis is enormous, even though such a crisis might be considered a once in a generation, or even once in a century, event. It is not difficult to see that a crisis that reduces output by between 5 percent and 10 percent for a number of years, and occurs once every fifty years, amounts to an annual cost several multiples of the revenue that will be generated by the UK bank levy (Haldane 2010). But how can we be certain of correctly establishing what the tax should be when we are trying to internalise costs that occur so infrequently? So although there is a sound case for a levy directed at the size of short-term borrowing, it would be foolish to regard that as the main tool to align costs and benefits of risky balance sheet activity.

If setting the appropriate price is hard, then some form of controls on quantities might be a better answer (Weitzman 1974). For example, limits on leverage have much to commend them. And for a generation, the quantitative control of this type that regulators have embraced was embodied in the capital standards set within the Basel framework. Last month a new concordat on such standards was reached in Basel – the so-called Basel III requirements. The challenge here is to set the requirements in a way that will materially affect the probability of a crisis.

Other forms of quantitative intervention include functional separation to reduce the costs of maturity transformation by ring-fencing those activities that we are most concerned to safeguard from disruption. If successful, the costs of any failure of financial institutions would be reduced. The challenge with this approach is to prevent the costs associated with the activity of maturity transformation from gravitating to another set of institutions – the 'shadow' banking system.

Whatever solution is adopted, the aim must be to align private and social costs.

Why Basel III is Not a Complete Answer

Lauded as a new standard, Basel III is seen by some as the answer to the failure of regulation to prevent the financial crisis. It is certainly a step in the right direction, an improvement on both Basel I and the ill-fated Basel II, and we should all welcome it. But if it is a giant leap for the regulators of the world, it is only a small step for mankind. Basel III on its own will not prevent another crisis for a number of reasons.

First, even the new levels of capital are insufficient to prevent another crisis. Calibrating required capital by reference to the losses incurred during the recent crisis takes inadequate account of the benefits to banks of massive government intervention and the implicit guarantee. More fundamentally, it fails to recognise that when sentiment changes only very high levels of capital would be sufficient to enable banks to obtain funding on anything like normal spreads to policy rates, as we can see at present. When investors change their view about the unknowable future – as they will occasionally in sudden and discontinuous ways – banks that were perceived as well-capitalised can seem under-capitalised with concerns over their solvency. That is what happened in 2007–8. As the IMF have pointed out, differences in capital ratios failed to predict which financial institutions would be vulnerable in the crisis (IMF 2009). Only very much higher levels of capital – levels that would be seen by the industry as wildly excessive most of the time – would prevent such a crisis.

Second, the Basel approach calculates the amount of capital required by using a measure of 'riskweighted' assets. Those risk weights are computed from past experience. Yet the circumstances in which capital needs to be available to absorb potential losses are precisely those when earlier judgements about the risk of different assets and their correlation are shown to be wrong. One might well say that a financial crisis occurs when the Basel risk weights turn out to be poor estimates of underlying risk. And that is not because investors, banks or regulators are incompetent. It is because the relevant risks are often impossible to assess in terms of fixed probabilities. Events can take place that we could not have envisaged, let alone to which we could attach probabilities. If only banks were playing in a casino then we probably could calculate appropriate risk weights. Unfortunately, the world is more complicated. So the regulatory framework needs to contain elements that are robust with respect to changes in the appropriate risk weights, and that is why the Bank of England advocated a simple leverage ratio as a key backstop to capital requirements.

Third, the Basel framework still focuses largely on the assets side of a bank's balance sheet. Basel II excluded consideration of the liquidity and liability structure of the balance sheet, so much so that when the UK adopted Basel II in 2007, of all the major banks the one with the highest capital ratio was, believe it or not, Northern Rock. Within weeks of announcing that it intended to return excess capital to its shareholders, Northern Rock ran out of money. Basel II was based on a judgement that mortgages were the safest form of lending irrespective of how they were financed. If a business model is based around a particular funding model that suddenly becomes unviable, then the business model becomes unviable too, as events in 2007 showed. Whether the measures included in Basel III will be able to deal properly with the risks that result from inadequate levels of liquid assets and a risky structure of liabilities remains to be seen.

One criticism of Basel III with which I have no truck is the length of the transition period. Banks have up to 2019 to adjust fully to the new requirements. Although some of the calculations of the alleged economic cost of higher capital requirements presented by the industry seem to me exaggerated (Institute of International Finance, 2010), I do believe that it is important in the present phase of de-leveraging not to exacerbate the challenge banks face in raising capital today. Banks should take advantage of opportunities to raise loss-absorbing capital, and should recognise the importance of using profits to rebuild capital rather than pay out higher dividends and compensation. But we must not forget the principle underlying the Basel approach: asking banks to maintain a buffer of capital above the minimum requirement allows them to run the buffer down in circumstances like the present. Rebuilding the buffer is a task for the future. So even though the Bank of England would have preferred an agreement to set capital ratios at higher levels in the long run, we have no intention of asking UK banks to adopt a faster timetable for implementation of Basel III. That logic should apply to any reforms we choose to implement. We should not expect to change the financial system for the better overnight. Rather we need radical reforms that will give us a much more robust system in the long run, accepting that it may take a period of many years to get there.

As with a bank levy, it is no criticism of Basel III to say that it is not a 'silver bullet'. The difficulty of identifying and calibrating the difference between the private and social costs of maturity transformation means that there is merit in having a basket of different measures to rein in excessive risk-taking. In the area of financial stability, it makes sense to have both belt and braces.

Large Institutions

The implicit subsidy to banks that are perceived as 'too important to fail' can be important to banks of any size but is usually seen as bigger for large institutions for which existing bank resolution procedures either do or could not apply. Moreover, most large complex financial institutions are global – at least in life if not in death. So a major international effort is underway to try to work out how best to deal with such institutions, initiated by heads of government at the G-20 Summit in Pittsburgh in 2009. Much of this work is being led by the Financial Stability Board. Ideas agreed in principle or under consideration include an addition to the Basel III capital requirement of an extra layer of either equity or other loss-absorbing capital, a special resolution regime for large institutions that would allow losses to be shared among creditors as well as equity-holders, and tentative steps towards international harmonisation of resolution procedures on which my colleague Paul Tucker and others are engaged.

Solving the 'too important to fail' problem will require ultimately that every financial sector entity can be left to fail without risk of threatening the functioning of the economy. So it is natural that improved resolution procedures are part of the overall strategy – and within many countries big steps forward have already been taken. But the successful resolution of a large institution would, in the absence of an implausibly large deposit insurance fund, require the ability to bail-in creditors. Yet that possibility would give an incentive to the bank to increase its dependence on short-term funding so that more creditors might get out in time. That might increase rather than decrease the fragility of the institution. So there would need to be restrictions on the maturity structure of its liabilities. Resolution would naturally go hand-in-hand with a greater reliance on instruments such as contingent capital. And there would be enormous challenges in resolving global banks that span countries with different legal jurisdictions. Extending resolution procedures to large institutions is a necessary but not sufficient condition for stability of the banking system.

More Radical Reforms

All of these potential reforms would be steps in the right direction. They would all help to put more of the costs of maturity mismatch on the shoulders of those who reap the benefits. But taxes, the Basel capital requirements, special arrangements for systemically important financial institutions and enhanced resolution procedures all have drawbacks and are unlikely to do the job perfectly. So, if we cannot rely solely on these types of measures, are there more fundamental directions in which we could move that would align costs and benefits more effectively?

One simple solution, advocated by my colleague David Miles, would be to move to very much higher levels of capital requirements – several orders of magnitude higher. A related proposal is to ensure there are large amounts of contingent capital in a bank's liability structure. Much more loss-absorbing capital – actual or contingent – can substantially reduce the size of costs that might be borne outside of a financial firm. But unless complete, capital requirements will never be able to guarantee that costs will not spill over elsewhere. This leads to the limiting case of proposals such as Professor Kotlikoff's idea to introduce what he calls 'limited purpose banking' (Kotlikoff 2010). That would ensure that each pool of investments made by a bank is turned into a mutual fund with no maturity mismatch. There is no possibility of alchemy. It is an idea worthy of further study.

Another avenue of reform is some form of functional separation. The Volcker Rule is one example. Another, more fundamental, example would be to divorce the payment system from risky lending activity – that is to prevent fractional reserve banking (for example, as proposed by Fisher 1936, Friedman 1960, Tobin 1987 and more recently by Ka, 2009).

In essence these proposals recognise that if banks undertake risky activities then it is highly dangerous to allow such 'gambling' to take place on the same balance sheet as is used to support the payments system, and other crucial parts of the financial infrastructure. And eliminating fractional reserve banking explicitly recognises that the pretence that risk-free deposits can be supported by risky assets is alchemy. If there is a need for genuinely safe deposits the only way they can be provided, while ensuring costs and benefits are fully aligned, is to insist such deposits do not coexist with risky assets.

The advantage of these types of more fundamental proposals is that no tax or capital requirement needs to be calibrated. And if successfully enforced then they certainly would be robust measures. But a key challenge is to ensure that maturity transformation does not simply migrate outside of the regulated perimeter, and end up benefiting from an implicit public subsidy (Tucker 2010b). That is difficult because it is the nature of the services – not the institutions – that is the concern. Ultimately, we need a system whereby the suppliers of funds to risky activities, whether intermediated via banks or any other entity, must understand that they will not be protected from loss by taxpayer bailouts. Creditors should know that they will bear losses in the event of failure.

We certainly cannot rely on being able to expand the scope of regulation without limit to prevent the migration of maturity mismatch. Regulators will never be able to keep up with the pace and scale of financial innovation. Nor should we want to restrict innovation. But it should be undertaken by investors using their own money not by intermediaries who also provide crucial services to the economy, allowing them to reap an implicit public subsidy. It will not be possible to regulate all parts of the financial system as if they were banks. As Jeffrey Lacker, President of the Federal Reserve Bank of Richmond, has argued, 'merely expanding the scope of regulation to chase those firms that extract implicit guarantees by engaging in maturity transformation would be an interminable journey with yet more financial instability in its wake' (Lacker 2010). In the end, clarity about the regulatory perimeter is both desirable and unavoidable – a task given to the Financial Policy Committee as part of the Bank of England's new responsibilities. And the attraction of the more radical solutions is that they offer the hope of avoiding the seemingly inevitable drift to ever more complex and costly regulation.

The broad answer to the problem is likely to be remarkably simple. Banks should be financed much more heavily by equity rather than short-term debt. Much, much more equity; much, much less short-term debt. Risky investments cannot be financed in any other way. What we cannot countenance is a continuation of the system in which bank executives trade and take risks on their own account, and yet those who finance them are protected from loss by the implicit taxpayer guarantees. The difficulty is in finding the right practical way to achieve that. Some of the solutions that economists have proposed have been dismissed by some as impractical and pie in the sky. But I am reminded of Keynes' dictum that 'practical men who believe themselves to be quite exempt from any intellectual influence are usually the slaves of some defunct economist' (Keynes 1936). Of all the many ways of organising banking, the worst is the one we have today.

I have suggested a number of ways in which the system could be reformed. But making the right choice will take much careful thought and a good deal of time. So I do not want today to offer a blueprint – and indeed that is for others to do. In the UK we are fortunate. The Independent Commission on Banking was set up earlier this year. It has outstanding members. I am sure they will lead us to the right solution, and I look forward to their findings.

Conclusions

There is no simple answer to the too important to fail nature of banks. Maturity transformation brings economic benefits but it creates real economic costs. The problem is that the costs do not fall on those who enjoy the benefits. The damaging externalities created by excessive maturity transformation and risk-taking must be internalised.

A market economy has proved to be the most reliable means for a society to expand its standard of living. But ever since the Industrial Revolution we have not cracked the problem of how to ensure a more stable banking system. We know that there will always be sharp and unpredictable movements in expectations, sentiment and hence valuations of financial assets. They represent our best guess as to what the future holds, and views about the future can change radically and unpredictably. It is a phenomenon that we must learn to live with.

But changes in expectations can create havoc with the banking system because it relies so heavily on transforming short-term debt into long-term risky assets. For a society to base its financial system on alchemy is a poor advertisement for its rationality.

Change is, I believe, inevitable. The question is only whether we can think our way through to a better outcome before the next generation is damaged by a future and bigger crisis. This crisis has already left a legacy of debt to the next generation. We must not leave them the legacy of a fragile banking system too.

I have explained the principles on which a successful reform of the system should rest. It is a programme that will take many years, if not decades. But, as Bagehot concluded in Lombard Street, 'I have written in vain if I require to say now that the problem is delicate, that the solution is varying and difficult, and that the result is inestimable to us all'.

The Ending of UK Exchange Control in 1979

Baron (Geoffrey) Howe of Aberavon, Chancellor of the Exchequer from 1979 to 1983 and Secretary of State for Foreign Affairs from 1983 to 1989 spoke to the Threadneedle Club in October 2010 on the historic decision to end UK Exchange Control in 1979. These complex controls, administered by a very large staff in the Bank of England, had been imposed in 1939 as an emergency measure to protect the UK economy through World War II. The decision helped restore freedom and flexibility to the City of London, which as a result enjoyed massive expansion through the 1980s.

PART THIRTEEN

An Innovative Banking Industry – Off the Deck and On Their Way

Angela Knight CBE

It was April 2007 when I took over as chief executive of the British Bankers' Association. I arrived from the rather quieter and calmer Association of Private Client Investment Managers and Stockbrokers, where I had been since the five extraordinarily turbulent years I spent as an MP and Minister in the Major government.

So I arrived at the BBA just in time for what feels like the most turbulent three years the banking industry has had for a century! Many have charted the run-up and causes of the credit crunch and the banking failures and, while only *some* of the banks made catastrophic errors, *all* bear a responsibility for dealing with the problems and creating a more stable and effective system.

I do not want to look back though.

I want to look to the future because that, after all, is where we are going. And at the moment, just about everything one can think of is up in the air for change. Internationally, the Basel capital and liquidity rules are under review; in the EU there are new supervisory authorities on crisis management proposals; and in the UK we have new regulatory authorities and responsibilities are shifting to the

Bank of England. These are just a few examples, and getting all these pieces settled into a coherent and well-operating pattern is absolutely vital.

So where are we now?

The G20 set off pretty well with some good strong statements about international co-ordination. They kicked into action New Work on the capital and liquidity that banks will have to hold. Coupled with better risk assessment, this package is known as 'Basel III'. But it has become clear that when it comes to enacting their agreements, the major financial centres of the world are not all in the same place. The USA will certainly make changes to its regulations. Dodd Frank will alter the dynamics, with some banks having some wholesale activities limited, so the shadow banking sector will doubtless grow as a result. More capital and liquidity will be required, but pay and bonuses meanwhile are likely to continue much as before. But will it be the full 'Basel III'?

In the Far East there is every sign that economic growth will continue faster than anywhere else. They will take notice of the various international agreements, but the degree of implementation will be tempered by a strong view that the credit crunch and subsequent problems were Western issues so it is the West that should be making changes.

The EU, meanwhile, is in a quandary. On the one hand it seeks to implement 'Basel III' and make other clear and coherent regulatory and structural changes through directives and rules right across Europe to provide a safer and more stable financial system. At the same time it has to handle the serious sovereign debt problems where the fiscal positions of some countries became strongly out of line with Euro zone monetary policy. These countries are now left with the consequences, which are chiefly cuts in public spending as they do not have the safety valve of being able to devalue their currency. Time will show how this develops.

The UK was very much in the spotlight – and a very negative spotlight – in the early days of the credit crunch. But now it has some opportunities, which have arisen due to three key factors. The first is that the new government has made its economic policy quite clear and as such the markets are convinced that the UK is going to deal properly with its budget deficit. Second, although the banking industry is still understandably publicly reviled, it is in the process of making very significant changes and is a willing partner in more reforms for stability, better governance and risk controls. These two things provide a springboard for financial services to rapidly recover, with the banks and the broader industry putting customers of all sizes and types at the core of their operation, so improving confidence both here and abroad.

The third factor that points towards opportunities for the UK is regulatory reform. The UK has both a large domestic banking industry and a huge international banking sector – and regulation makes an essential contribution to the whole picture. Collectively the UK banking industry has long provided the finance for mortgages and small businesses; for large and international institutions; and for governments and projects around the world. Regulation needs to be appropriate and relevant to all of these. But the whole industry – both domestic and international – is not surprisingly judged by people's personal experiences in branches, on the telephone or over the internet because it is difficult to explain, for example, what is a structured financial product for an international company or indeed why such a thing matters.

The banking industry in the UK operates 120 million accounts so it is bound to make mistakes – and with an unstable retail regulatory regime those mistakes can be exaggerated. But even more importantly the ability to resolve them can be impeded, which shows how crucial regulation is. It is far from an arcane and dry subject as it provides the framework in which a free market can operate both at home and abroad.

Current proposals in the field of regulatory reform put a lot more responsibility back to the Bank of England. Some call this restoring to the Bank its historic role, but in reality the Bank will be given a lot more powers than it has had for a great many years.

In 1997 the Bank lost its role for regulating banks but gained responsibility for monetary policy. It is now proposed that the Bank retains monetary policy responsibilities; becomes the prudential regulator of the banking industry (and also building societies and insurers); has oversight of payments; is the 'resolution authority' (has formal powers to intervene and sort out a bank if it gets into difficulty); and is the macro-prudential supervisor. In actual fact, the Bank of England does a lot of this in some form already. But now its role will be given absolute clarity by being formally codified in law. Much will be written about this and no doubt there will be many arguments, too, as the new legislation goes through its parliamentary processes.

So far, little critical attention has been paid to the Bank's new macro-prudential role. This will be executed through a Financial Policy Committee (FPC) and means that the Bank will be able to take early action if it sees a bubble forming or the economy racing ahead too fast. Instead of just having the ability to raise or lower interest rates, it will be able to raise capital requirements to limit the provision of credit or reduce the loan-to-value ratios for a mortgage. These tools clearly have a significant economic and socio-economic potential. Therefore the decision making process behind them, as well as their actual use, must ensure an economic balance is achieved and that any changes take into account international competitiveness.

Judgement in this area as in many others is essential. We need to see good judgement in regulating; good judgement in supervision; and good judgement in fiscal, monetary and macro-prudential decision making.

My short few years in the banking industry feel like a lifetime – not least because there has been a lifetime's worth of ups and downs, changes and decisions to be made! I am a believer, though, in an innovative banking industry. The banks are now off the deck and on their way, and look forward to working in partnership with the Bank of England. Sensible, clear, careful and high-quality regulation and supervision has the right feel about it.

Photograph by Stephen Tempest

MORE STRONG GALES IMMINENT?

Possibly from the East

PART FOURTEEN

Prospects and Opportunities for Central Banks

There are 162 central banks in operation today, one for almost every country in the world. They employ some 350,000 people. The cornerstone and prime model of central banking worldwide is the Bank of England. Others, such as the Swedish Riksbank, founded in 1668 or the Federal Reserve System of the United States launched in 1913, have legitimate claims to fame, but the historical pre-eminence of the Bank of England rests on a continuity of operation in London, under many definitions still the largest financial centre in the world.

In central banking terms, as in commerce and foreign trade, London's record is unsurpassed as a global market hub, and the Bank of England holds pole position as a seasoned survivor of many financial crises and attacks on its integrity.

The Bank of England's claim to pre-eminence rests primarily and essentially on its position as an innovator in the history of the development of money, credit, exchange trading and government financing. From the outset in 1694, it was able to raise massive finance from the merchants of London to equip and pay the British Army then fighting in Flanders and to build new dockyards and ships for the Royal Navy. Quickly, it multiplied the use of paper money, widened the scope of trade finance and reinforced the value and quality of the coinage in circulation. An Act of Parliament in 1844 gave the Bank a monopoly in the issue of banknotes, and in 1873 it ushered in the adoption of the Gold Standard, which persisted until World War One and which was revived for a time in the 1920s.

'As Safe as the Bank of England'

In populist political terms worldwide, the Bank's almost unblemished record of probity, prudence and an ability to act swiftly, discreetly and effectively has, to this day, provided a guarantee of trust, goodwill, honourable dealing and, above all, wise and prudent management.The Bank of England remains a central icon of the international financial system, on which all global investment, development and trade depends.

What Do Central Bankers Think They Are Doing?

There is in fact a lot of diversity in the way the world's central banks go about their business. A study of 47 leading central banks published by the Swedish Riksbank in 2006 asked each of them to define their objectives. 21 of them (46 percent) put Price Stability as their prime objective. The study went on to ask what were their objectives, apart from monetary policy. Roughly half signed up to Financial Stability and the soundness of the financial system. A smaller proportion, about a quarter of them cited broader economic objectives such as maintaining economic growth, expanding employment and defending the exchange rate. Roughly 40 percent described their exchange-rate policy as free-floating, although this description has been challenged in many cases. The number of central banks stating that they were pegged to the dollar was matched by the same number declaring they were pegged to the euro. On financial regulation, some 120 central banks undertake some aspect of hands-on regulation:

about 60 percent (97 in number) say they supervise banks and 40 percent (65 in number) say they do not. China is one state where bank supervision is not carried out by the central bank, so, in population terms, the globe is roughly equally divided between those with a central bank that supervises the banks and those with a central bank that does not.

International Co-ordination

Three international organisations now lead the field in global co-operation in central banking, but the Bank of England has over the last five years greatly strengthened its position as the global role model, innovator and No.1 practical training, education and advice centre for the rest.

- **The Bank for International Settlements**

  The BIS was founded in Basel, Switzerland in 1930 with a primary mandate of resolving the complex problems of settling post-World War One reparations.Since then it has been the focal consultation point for the key central bank governors and presidents and their senior staff. By brilliant diplomacy, it survived World War Two intact despite being primarily dependent on income from the German Reichsbank. More recently, it has grown into a centre of excellence on global economics as well as on central banking analysis and practice with a highly qualified international staff. Today it has a pivotal role in the formulation of new prudential rules for the global banking system. Its Basel III proposals now on the table may not be enshrined in statute in time to prevent further major crises, and may need supplementing with greater powers and commitment by governments as well as by central banks. But there is general consensus, albeit somewhat qualified in the United States that the BIS is on the right track.

- **The International Monetary Fund**

  The IMF was created at the Bretton Woods Conference held near Washington DC in 1944. In the post-war years it rapidly established its role as prime source of massive interim finance for countries in acute budgetary, balance of payments or institutional crisis, lending only on conditions of compliance to a package of rescue measures designed to restore the borrower to sound economic and financial health. In the 1970s and 1980s, these demands for help came thick and fast but were increasingly accompanied by a reluctance to impose the levels of deflation set by the IMF. By the 1990s a strong counter-current of criticism by developing countries that the IMF rescue packages were in fact devices to export heavy pollutant and other unwanted industries from the industrialised world and a means to restrain the legitimate aspirations of the third world for strong economic growth, began to take a toll. Latterly, however, despite widespread pleas that the old Bretton Woods institutions in Washington DC were reaching the end of their useful lives, the IMF, World Bank and the International Finance Corporation (IFC) have all reacted strongly to the lack of agreement on any successor institutions and recently, under the stimulus of the 2007–9 financial crisis, have all taken on a fresh lease of life.

- **The Financial Stability Board**

  The FSB is the third and most recent lead player in the game. It derives from the Financial Stability Forum set up in 1999 in the wake of the Asian financial crisis of 1997–8. Its first Chairman was Andrew Crockett, ex-Bank of England and then General Manager of the Bank for International Settlements, which has provided the

Secretariat. Membership has now been extended to all members of the G20.

Co-operation Between the BIS, IMF and FSB

A major lesson from the 2007 to 2009 financial crisis is that co-operation between the key international financial agencies and the world's leading banks was seen to fail. There were plenty of warnings of misused assets, the limitations on customer protection, a gambling mentality pervading the investment arms of some banks,the likely consequences of real-estate speculation and of uncontrollable credit bubbles. Yet the national and international authorities were perplexed as to how to react. In the United Kingdom, the separation between the Bank of England and the Financial Services Authority in 1997 was widely blamed.

Secrecy, Discretion and Transparency

Traditionally, as expounded elsewhere in this book, central banks like the Bank of England have relied on a close face-to-face monitoring of the market to know where problems might develop and to work out solutions in advance. Notorious for their enigmatic responses and refusals to answer delicate questions from the press, politicians and the general public, successive Governors of the Bank of England have been extremely careful to maintain a high level of secrecy. But times change, and the pressure for maximum transparency and public understanding is very high indeed. Here again, Mervyn King and his team have led the way in a new direction. Chapters 7 and 12 of this book give extracts from Mervyn King's recent speeches in September and October 2010 to the Trade Union Congress in Manchester and the Buttonwood Gathering in New York. Both reflect an impressive grasp of the fundamentals and a meticulous attention to detail. I have read through in the Information Centre of the Bank all the texts of the Governors' speeches from 1953 to 2003 – not a single one approaches the clarity and logic and sheer readability of Mervyn King. Once again, the Bank of England has cut new ground, devoting immense effort to explain to the best of their ability what is happening, and likely to happen and where the opportunities and pitfalls might lie ahead.

An Agenda For Change

'Central banks are in cultural transition. The past model – a secretive institution little inclined to explain itself and maintaining an air of mystery, cloaked in constructive ambiguity, and led by a philosopher king – has run its course. The new model central bank will be more accountable, transparent and frank about the limitations of its powers. It will be led by an individual who is skilled in chairmanship and communication and who has a deep understanding (and experience) of the financial sector and the wider economy on a global scale. Taciturn autocrats need no longer apply.'

(This is the final paragraph of the final chapter under the above heading of Banking on the Future – The Fall and Rise of Central Banks *by Sir Howard Davies and David Green published in 2010 by Princeton University Press.*

PART FIFTEEN

The Future of the Bank – A Silver Lining?

Paul Tempest

All over the United Kingdom, the deliverability of the 'pound in your pocket' has not been in much doubt, at least not since the establishment of the Bank of England in 1694. Whether in the form of gold sovereigns, silver shillings or other coins, notes of many denominations or bank balances used at home and in trade worldwide, the pound sterling has had to endure wild fluctuations on the exchanges, massive note forgery, swingeing exchange control, bank implosions, government edicts of dubious origin or intent and many other indignities. The point is that, over this very long period, sterling and the Bank of England have endured, even under the toughest of conditions such as those of the past three to four years. Yet sterling and the Bank of England are not invincible and there are many in Europe who would be very happy to see both swallowed up by the Euro and the European Central Bank.

'As Safe as the Bank of England'

For the public, the image of a fortress built on a bedrock of bullion surrounded by a sea of paper and cyber-money and protected by ancient, high blank walls is deeply engrained. They expect the Bank of England to last for ever. The Bank of England's future must surely be as safe as the Bank of England has been so far. Nothing could be more misleading.

It is not inconceivable (although now increasingly unlikely) that the British Government could be persuaded or coerced to join the Eurozone and abandon sterling. Management of the Euro rests with the European Central Bank and there would not be much left for the Bank of England to do, apart from the functions of local agent, distributor and monitor of the Euro, much of which could be eventually outsourced.

A Question of Human Resources

Through the period 2007 to 2010, the Bank of England has passed through one of the greatest financial crises in its history – certainly comparable to the financial meltdown of the Napoleonic Wars or the Great Depression of the 1930s. It did so in a weakened condition following the Labour Government's surprise decision in 1997 to hand over banking supervision accountability to a new Financial Services Authority without providing adequate arrangements for swift and decisive action as soon as any bank or other financial institution showed signs of running into trouble. While the staff of the FSA grew towards the 2,500 mark, the Bank of England staff list was being shrunk and even in 2007, it recorded a further fall of 5 percent in staff numbers. Retrenchment on this scale to a low-point of around 1,550 where a large number are on short-term contracts, has cut away or outsourced some of the accumulated wisdom of the Bank, so highly valued in its heyday by both the City and the Government.

There were, however, compensating benefits. This rigorous reappraisal of the Bank's role was in some ways overdue and has, of course, had benefits in terms of modernisation, computerisation and other enhanced efficiency. Yet it became clear that the pendulum had swung too far, below the critical mass necessary to generate adequate central banking skills for the longer term. Since 2008 staff numbers have again begun to rise. The new staff needs recruitment on stable terms and with adequate incentives, training and promotion opportunities and rewards. A plan is needed to identify these expanding opportunities and to provide prompt budgetary provision to finance and underpin a long-term human resources strategy of this nature.

A Strong, Enduring Link with the Treasury

HM Treasury has always recognised the Bank's traditional strengths both in relations with and the financing of the public sector and in a close understanding of how the City works and thinks. Even today, the Treasury accepts that the Bank enjoys a dimension of experience and expertise that the Treasury would not expect to be able to acquire but which can complement Whitehall and provide strong support for government.

One important point is that the Bank of England, unlike all Government spending departments, has never been a drain on the Exchequer. It generates ample earnings from the markets to finance its own activities and any expansion needed. Indeed any expansion of Bank activities in the markets will bring a rise in the large surplus paid over each year to the Exchequer.

City-Bank Relations Need Strengthening

At the domestic level, there are two urgent interrelated priorities for the immediate future. The first is a need for an all-round strengthening of warm face-to-face Bank of England relations with the City in general and with the banking sector in particular. The decision of the Coalition Government to disband the Financial Services Authority (FSA) and restore responsibility for bank supervision to the Bank in 2012 will assist in this process, but it is essential that the Bank of England sets its own terms for this transformation and that it does not merely take over the rule-book, staff structure and statistical procedures of the FSA. Above all, the Bank has to provide reassurance to the Government, to the banking sector and to the general public that it is again fully equipped to act promptly, effectively and, where necessary, discreetly to achieve its objectives of financial stability.

Monetary Policy Needs Some Rethinking

The second priority for the immediate future is to supplement and reinforce the anti-inflationary mechanism whereby the government sets a target rate of inflation and then leaves it to the Bank to deliver the correct result by adjusting its interest rate. Under present conditions of high unemployment, low economic growth and a continuing credit freeze, low interest rates have yet to deliver the certainty of future economic growth. Some of our wisest observers are beginning to point out the risks in prolonging unnecessarily cuts in public sector spending and of installing a too punitive fiscal regime. The issue here is one of mood. Restored economic growth will ease the pressures of debt management. Here we have some good news: a corner has been turned. UK economic growth in 2010, although modest at 2 percent, is about double what was predicted a year earlier. Confidence and optimism are absolutely essential if we are to put the misery of the financial crisis of 2007-9 firmly behind us, so that the UK can begin to rebuild a dynamic, high-growth economy founded on wide public understanding and endorsement. There is also very good news from the City of London.

The City of London is Sure of Imminent Resurgence

As explained in the later chapters of this book, the City of London is already mobilising to take advantage of the threadbare policies of the rest of the European Community – clumsy restrictive regulation, the straitjacket of Euro-zone membership, high state indebtedness and a growing reluctance of the richer states to bail out the weaker economies. What the City of London has to offer in abundance in these circumstances are the advantages of the largest and most flexible and most innovative financial centre in the world. This position at the top will be constantly challenged in each sector of the market, but the economies of scale of some of the largest London financial and commodity exchanges, their record for reliability and their stable procedures under the rule of law will again weigh heavily in London's favour.

This brings me to the fundamental conclusion of this book. The surmounting of the 2007–10 financial crisis is, for the Bank of England, a success story. Action was taken promptly. After Northern Rock, to the surprise of the jeremiahs, the banks of the United Kingdom remained in business. There was no meltdown in the markets and the global payments system survived more or less intact. All this presents an immense global opportunity for the Bank of England today.

The International Status of the Bank of England

Since the 1920s the Bank has evolved into a major player on the world financial scene, at least the equal in influence of its peers like the Federal Reserve Bank system of the United States or the European Central Bank. Since 1997, it has been able to demonstrate worldwide that the length and depth of its experience in the international financial and economic spheres is second to none.

The Challenge of the Eurozone

Within this context, the future path of monetary union within the expanded European Community poses particular dilemmas for the UK. So far the Bank of England has been wholly consistent in advancing the conviction that monetary union can only proceed where fiscal policy coordination is on a parallel track in all the member states. Sadly, fiscal alignment is in acute disarray. Divergences in the competitiveness of these eurozone states can no longer be expressed by fluctuations in the value of each state's own currency. All are bound, willy nilly, to the wheel of the Euro as common currency. Over the past year these tensions have put into question the very survival of the Euro. Survive it probably will but only at heavy cost to the major players faced with bailing out the weaker states.

While the rest of Europe carries great importance for the Bank and it listens carefully to the views of the Deutsche Bundesbank, Banque de France, Nederlandsche Bank, the Banca d'Italia and other European central banks, the focus of the Bank of England has always been much wider, a comprehensive global vision. The rest of the world knows this. There is no need for the Old Lady to advertise and sell her services. They are all in high demand. In this context, the Bank has achieved a great deal over the last five years. I will begin with the highly successful Centre for Central Banking Studies located in the Bank in Threadneedle Street.

A Centre of Excellence for Trainee Central Bankers

Over the last five years a new foundation, the Centre for Central Banking Studies in the Bank of England has been laid for training central bankers from all over the world – 1,520 participants from 139 central banks in 2008 with slightly lower figures for 2009, reflecting the increased workloads of central banks as the 2007–9 financial crisis began to take its toll. For further details, see Annex 5. Sessions are held in London (570 participants in 2009) or overseas (615 in 2009). There is sustained demand for these courses. Out of them have come regular professional consultations with China, India, Brazil, Indonesia, the Russian Federation and a long list of developing countries. It would not be fanciful to imagine that with time this massive training effort and consultation process will blossom into a fully-fledged university or specialised college of high world repute, based in London or elsewhere in the United Kingdom and specialising in global finance, trade and investment.

An Open Door for the General Public

As a counterpart to this activity the Bank of England Museum has further developed its coverage of the contemporary scene, receiving hundreds of visitors each day from home and overseas and, over each month, several thousand schoolchildren in escorted groups. All are given comprehensive oral and written briefing and some idea of what the Bank of England provides today. Each visitor, for example, can take hold of a gold bullion ingot and try to lift it. There are ingenious hands-on models to demonstrate how inflation can be controlled and the impact of interest rates on the real economy. Entry to the Museum is free; visitors are warmly welcomed; gallery assistants are trained and briefed to answer questions.

From this highly successful information base, it may be possible to add on a more comprehensive extensive research centre in the adjoining banking halls or elsewhere. This could provide, say for the general public, state-of-the art and right up-to-date presentations on the state of the UK and global economy, the outlines of the UK and global banking system and even a structured guide to the rest of the financial sector in the UK. Placed in the context of rising global population and pressures on food, water, energy and other mineral resources, this may help to publicise the broader, long-term concerns of the Bank and the UK and to convey the Bank of England's enhanced understanding of the key global issues. The need to maintain the momentum of new technology in the UK and elsewhere to provide more robust patterns of industrial production and international trade, the progress made in cutting unemployment and under-employment, and efforts to diversify energy sources and enhance energy utilisation might, for example, feature in the film and video programmes.

All such services and activities provide tangible evidence that the Bank of England is no longer a mysterious, remote, silent organisation, barred to the outside world. Access to a wide range of up-to-date information about the Bank is available at any time of the day or night and anywhere in the world through the Internet. Recently, considerable thought has been deployed on how to reinforce these services with a continuing commentary on the latest financial news, trends and other developments and more detailed coverage of global trends and prospects.

Transparency and a Lively Critique

The need for increased transparency in the financial sector of every economy worldwide is reflected in the Bank's rapid development of its statistical base and its comprehensive coverage of all parts of the UK through its twelve regional Agents and their staffs. Its eloquence in analysing the present situation and prospects has improved by leaps and bounds: there are few other central banks in the world that are capable of analysing and identifying, not only their national interest but also the global outcomes, options and opportunities. Almost all, however, are keen to tap into this global centre of expertise.

At a formal level, the Bank's publications available on-line and in printed format have been extensively developed. A starting point is the Annual Report published in May each year and supplemented by the four Quarterly Reports which include a wide range of statistics together with guest articles and texts of speeches and papers by the Governors and senior officials. For those following the proceedings of the Monetary Policy Committee, the regular series of

Inflation Reports provide essential background.

The media are briefed thoroughly after each meeting of the Monetary Policy Committee and transcripts of the meetings are made available to the press as soon as possible, once they have been thoroughly checked for any errors in the recording process. Panels of university professors and researchers and prominent City analysts are regularly invited into the Bank to question the officials involved and to express their own opinions. This provides a continuous, helpful and lively critique of all Bank policy decisions.

The Heart of the Matter – Turning the Corner

There is undeniable evidence in this book and elsewhere that the Bank of England has just turned a major corner. Over the past three years of the global financial crisis, it has not only survived, but, battle-hardened, it has prospered. Now, there are major new tasks and challenges facing the Bank.

First, we must recognise that the world is changing rapidly. Within my own lifetime, while the global population has all but tripled, the UK has moved from imperial and colonial mode through the high cost and bleak consequences of World War II. Then followed the British frustration at being pushed aside by the USA and the Soviet Union in the Cold War, and, later, the realisation that the astonishing post-war growth of Germany and Japan was forcing the UK further down the pecking order. The collapse of the Soviet Union in 1989 left the USA as principal global policeman for the next twenty years, but its role as principal motor of global economic growth had already been steadily eroded by the South Eastern tigers, increasingly challenged by China and by the expansion of the European economies and also by newcomers such as Brazil, Turkey and India. Now, as we begin to pass from the uni-polar world of US leadership into a non-polar world where the leading states are in serious danger of becoming more preoccupied with their own domestic agendas, social turbulence emanating from frustrated expectations and in diverting competitive energies into securing their borders, expanding their export markets and tying down the sources of their imports, what the deeply interdependent world needs is an image of restored stability, enhanced international co-operation and an icon of globalisation. Where better to look for it than in the Bank of England, already an acknowledged centre of excellence?

Quality of Service and Proven Reliability

The diminution of the UK's ability to influence other states directly is, astonishingly, out of line with the rapid growth of the City of London. How can this be? We have no longer any political means to force independent states to shop in London for their financial needs. They come to us, as in any free market, attracted by the quality of service, the economies of scale, the low costs and the proven reliability of our system. English is the global language of international trade and finance. Indeed our financial procedures established over centuries are now a welcome reassurance of stability. The fact that we no longer try to control one quarter of the world population or interfere in their internal affairs is a relief not only to everyone else, but also to ourselves. In a nutshell, the UK has become more welcoming, less demanding, more international. It is a better listener than, say, China, Russia or even the USA. It is here that a great opportunity lies for the future.

I have tried in this book to emphasise that the painful experiences of the financial crisis of 2007–10 will be seen to have done much good, in having flushed out some of the scoundrels and forcing us to revisit the fundamentals of our society and culture. The rest of the world will broadly welcome the wise, old-fashioned, respectable, friendly ways of the British, and have no good reason to fear colonial or any other maltreatment at their hands.

At the heart of the City of London stands the Bank of England with an unequalled and unbroken three-century record of honest, straightforward dealing and an immense empathy with the rest of the world. It is widely revered and listened to. The world's bankers and central bankers stream in and out of the main entrance in Threadneedle Street; the Bank staff are to be found all over the world when invited to provide professional advice and above all, they listen carefully. By e-mail and mobile telephone backed by more conventional communications, problem-solving worldwide has become quicker and easier. By 2040, say the Bank for International Settlements, advances in telecommunications and adherence to a simple common set of rules may have overcome the hurdles and barriers to instant global data collection that have previously slowed up the emergence of a simple, day-to-day, largely automatic global regulatory process.

A Global Focus Point

The Bank of England is today very well-placed to become a global focus point: a key hub as well as a worldwide icon in this new international system. Yet there is something that the Bank can bring to the table that is without price. It is not only the accumulated moral imperative of fair dealing, but also a longstanding awareness that the long-term national interest has always been to embrace the long-term regional and global interest. The preservation of peace; the elimination of war; the suppression of mindless global terrorism; the economic interdependence of free, independent states; freedom of travel and speech and other basic human rights, the progressive elimination of poverty, environmental protection, a sustainable use of resources, ample clean water, food, shelter, clothing, electricity for all – these all depend on an innate optimism of building a better, interconnected world.

In the psychology of global banking which can only be built on confidence and trust at all levels, the new independence of the Bank of England exemplified by the creation of the Monetary Policy Committee in 1997 is a most important pointer in the right direction.

A Silver Lining

A lesson to be learned from the past 14 years is that the UK has derived immense benefit from preserving flexibility in economic and monetary management, a point not lost on the world's central bankers who bring substantial reserve, exchange and investment business to London on account of this flexibility and capacity. It is very difficult to see how we could ever wish to forego this freedom and manoeuvrability in favour of a foreign yoke. Changes expected in the global markets and in the balance between the western and eastern hemispheres will need constant adjustment by the likes of the Bank of England. As the balance swings inexorably towards the East, there may be renewed bouts of acute turbulence in the markets, exacerbated by political, possibly military intervention. In this evolving world, we will need a strong and independent Bank of England to help see us through. The immediate task is to restore its strength and flexibility and to rebuild strong and cordial relations both with the City of London and worldwide.

Ahead lie many storms, dark clouds and great uncertainties. In my opinion, the Bank of England is well-equipped and ready to play a vital role. Also it can provide an enduring image of hope, stability, reliability and practical common sense in the rapid globalisation of the financial markets that is already beginning to affect us all – a vital silver lining, a familiar and welcome beacon and an icon in the process, shared by everyone and every state, in building together a better world.

ANNEX 1

Governors of the Bank of England 1907–2011

1907–09	William Middleton Campbell
1909–11	Reginald Eden Johnston
1911–13	Alfred Clayton Cole
1913–18	Walter Cunliffe
1918–20	Brien Cokayne
1920–44	Montagu Collet Norman
1944–49	Thomas Sivewright Catto
1949–61	Cameron Fromanteel Cobbold
1961–66	Rowland Stanley George Baring, the Earl of Cromer
1966–73	Leslie Kenneth O'Brien
1973–83	Gordon William Humphreys Richardson
1983–93	Robert (Robin) Leigh-Pemberton
1993–2003	Edward Alan John George
2003–	Mervyn Allister King

ANNEX 2

Members of the Court of the Bank of England at 1 January 2011

Mervyn King	Governor
Charlie Bean	Deputy Governor
Paul Tucker	Deputy Governor
Sir David Lees	Chairman of the Court
Brendan Barber	General Secretary, Trades Union Congress
Roger Carr	Chairman, Centrica plc
Lady (Susan) Rice CBE	Managing Director, Lloyds Banking Group (Scotland)
Lord (Adair) Turner	Chairman, Financial Services Authority
Antonio Horton-Osorio	Chief Executive, Santander UK
Mark Tucker	Board Member, Edinburgh Festival Centre Ltf
Harrison Young	Chairman, NBN Co Ltd
John Stewart	Chairman, Legal & General Group

The 18 members of the Court at 1 March 2008 are listed in Annex 2 of The Bank of England Bedside Book Volume 1 – A Thread of Gold *published by Stacey International, London in October 2008.*

ANNEX 3

The Bank of England Executive Team at 1 January 2011

Mervyn King	Governor
Charlie Bean	Deputy Governor Monetary Policy
Paul Tucker	Deputy Governor Financial Stability
Andrew Bailey	Executive Director Banking Services & Chief Cashier
Spencer Dale	Executive Director Monetary Analysis & Statistics
Paul Fisher	Executive Director Markets
John Footman	Executive Director Central Services & Secretary of the Bank
Andy Haldane	Executive Director Financial Stability
Warwick Jones	Finance Director
Graham Nicholson	Chief Legal Adviser
Jenny Scott	Executive Director Communications
Catherine Brown*	Executive Director Human Resources

**from 17 January 2011*

ANNEX 4

Members of the Bank of England Monetary Policy Committee at 1 January 2011

		Appointed until
Mervyn King	Governor	30.6.13
Charlie Bean	Deputy Governor	30.6.13
Paul Tucker	Deputy Governor	28.2.14

The Two Bank of England Executive Directors

Spencer Dale	Executive Director	31.5.13
Paul Fisher	Executive Director	31.5.11

The Four External Members Appointed by the Chancellor

Professor David Miles	31.5.12
Dr Adam Posen	31.8.12
Dr Andrew Sentance	31.5.11
Dr Martin Weale	31.7.13

A representative of the Treasury also sits with the Committee at its meetings.

ANNEX 5

The Twelve Regional Agents of the Bank of England at 1 January 2011

Peter Andrews	Greater London
Neil Ashbridge	Wales
Stephen Collins	South West
Graeme Chaplin	West Midlands & Oxfordshire
Alastair Cunningham	East Midlands
William Dowson	Scotland
Phil Eckersley	South East & East Anglia
Paul Fullerton	Yorkshire & The Humber
Frances Hill	Northern Ireland
Chris Piper	Central Southern England
Rosie Smith	North East
John Young	North West

ANNEX 6

The Centre for Central Banking Studies in the Bank of England Activities 2007–9

	2007	2008	2009
London Events			
Number of London Events	27	26	27
Number of Participants	608	556	570
International Events			
Number of International Events	37	30	23
Number of Participants	916	964	615
Total numbers			
of participants	1,524	1,520	1,185
of central banks	138	139	125

International Seminars and Workshops were held in 2009 in Armenia, Austria, El Salvador, Indonesia, Lithuania, Namibia, Papua New Guinea, Philippines (with representatives of 11 South-East Asia countries plus Australia, India and Bangladesh) on one course and central bankers from 13 South East Asia countries on another separate course), Russia, Serbia, Sierra Leone (with 22 representatives from Ghana, Gambia, Liberia, Nigeria and Sierra Leone), Tanzania (with representatives from Burundi, Kenya, Rwanda, Tanzania and Uganda), Ukraine (with participants from Armenia, Belarus, Czech Republic, Georgia, Latvia, Russia, Moldova, Poland, Tajikistan and Ukraine), the United Arab Emirates (with participants from Algeria, Iraq, Jordan, Kuwait, Lebanon, Morocco, Oman, Palestine, Qatar and Saudi Arabia) and the United States. Seminars in London included (annual) China, EU (France, Germany, Netherlands); representatives of Asian central banks in London, with two seminars for the Reserve Bank of India. CCBS Handbooks are also available in Arabic, Russian and Spanish.

ANNEX 7

Threadneedle Club Annual Dinner Lead Guests of Honour

1. 1986	**Lord Richardson**, Governor	1973–83
2. 1987	**Lord O'Brien**, Governor	1966–73
3. 1988	**Sir Hector Laing**, Director	1973–91
4. 1989	**Sir Adrian Cadbury**, Director	1970–94
5. 1990	**Rodney Galpin**, Director	1984–88
6. 1991	**Sir George Blunden**, Deputy Governor	1986–90
7. 1992	**Lord Kingsdown**, Governor	1983–93
8. 1993	**Sir Jeremy Morse**, Director	1965–72 & 93–97
9. 1994	**Lord George**, Governor	1993–03
10. 1995	**Sir Kit McMahon**, Deputy Governor	1980–85
11. 1996	**Brian Quinn**, Director	1988–96
12. 1997	**Tony Coleby**, Director	1990–94
13. 1998	**Lord George**, Governor	1993–03
14. 1999	**Ian Plenderleith**, Director	1994–02
15. 2000	**Michael Foot**, Director	1996–98
16. 2001	**Malcolm Gill**, Chief Cashier	1988–91
17. 2002	**Mervyn King**, Governor	since 2003
18. 2003	**Pen Kent**, Director	1994–97
19. 2004	**Lord George**, Governor	1993–03
20. 2005	**Sir Howard Davies**, Deputy Governor	1995–97
21. 2006	**Rt Hon Lord Lawson of Blaby**, Chancellor of the Exchequer	1983–89
	Admiral Sir Jeremy de Halpert, Deputy Master, Trinity House	since 2002
22. 2007	**Andrew Bailey**, Chief Cashier/Director	since 2003
	Garth Hewitt, Editor, *The Old Lady*	1996–2007
23. 2008	**Rt Hon Lord Lamont of Lerwick**, Chancellor of the Exchequer	1990–93
	Admiral Sir Jeremy de Halpert, Deputy Master, Trinity House	
24. 2009	**Sir John Parker**, Chairman of the Court	2004–09
	Charlie Bean, Deputy Governor	since 2009
	Prof. Forrest Capie, Historian of the Bank	since 2004
25. 2010	**Sir David Walker**, Chairman, Morgan Stanley Int'l	since 2004
	Rt Hon Baron Howe of Aberavon,	
	Chancellor of the Exchequer	1979–83
	Secretary of State for Foreign Affairs	1983–89
	Baroness Howe of Idlicote, Chairman of the Broadcasting Standards Commission	1997–99
	Rt Hon Lord Lawson of Blaby,	
	Secretary of State for Energy	1981–83

Paul Tempest, Chairman: Gavin Gordon, Secretary

The Threadneedle Club is open to anyone who has worked in the Bank of England in any capacity for more than one year. For details, please contact the Secretary, Gavin Gordon on 01784 482365.

Bibliography

Acres, M., *The Bank of England from Within*, Oxford University Press, 1931

Bagehot, W., *A Description of the Money Market*, Henry S King, London, 1873

BIS, Basel, *Issues in the Governance of Central Banks*, Bank for International Settlements, Basel, 2009

Blair, T., *A Journey*, Hutchinson, London, 2010

Brown, G., *Beyond the Crash*, Simon & Schuster, London, New York, Sydney, Toronto, 2010

Capie, F., *The Bank of England 1950s to 1979*, Cambridge University Press, 2010

——, Goodhart, C., Fischer, S., Schnadt, N., *The Future of Central Banking*, Cambridge University Press, 1994

Davies, H., Green, D., *Banking on the Future – The Fall and Rise of Central Banks*, Princeton University Press, 2010

——, Green, D., *Global Financial Regulation*, Polity Press, Chichester, UK, 2008

Hennessy, E., *A Domestic History of the Bank of England 1930–1960*, Cambridge University Press, 1992

Keynes, J.M., *The General Theory of Employment, Interest and Money*, Cambridge University Press,1936

Lawson, N., *Memoirs of a Tory Radical*, Biteback Publishing, UK, 2010

Marsh, D., *The Euro – The Politics of the New Global Currency*, Yale University Press, 2009

Tempest, P., *The Bank of England – A Thread of Gold 1694–2008*, Stacey International, London, 2008

——, *An Umbrella for the Old Lady*, Teapot Press, London, 2004

——, *The Old Lady Overseas*, Teapot Press, London, 2002

Toniolo, G., *Central Bank Cooperation at the Bank for International Settlements*, Cambridge University Press, 2005

Turner, A., *A Regulatory Response to the Global Banking Crisis*, Financial Services Authority, London, 2009

Wiggin, A., Incontera, K., *IOUSA – One Nation, Under Stress, In Debt*, John Wiley & Sons, Hoboken, NJ, 2008

Summary Index of People and Events in Volume One of The Bank of England Bedside Book – A Thread of Gold (2008)

Summary Index of People and Events in Volume Two The Bank of England - A Silver Lining?